Daddy's Love Notes

Daddy's Love Notes

...a bit of light for the end of your torch

Bashon Mann

Dedicated to Basil & Sabine, my greatest gift

ISBN: 0692549099
ISBN 13: 9780692549094

Introduction

THEY SAY IMITATION is the greatest form of flattery, though if you're not careful it can lead to copyright infringement. A few years ago I watched closely as several of my friends used social media to highlight significant moments in their lives as they approached the milestone age of 40. I found this to be a typically intriguing way to look back and savor the special events and people that helped shape their lives. It seemed to serve as a visual reminder of the poignant moments in their younger years, perhaps reaffirming for them not to take life for granted as they began the "back 9" of life. The more I watched these posts, these collections of memories, I began to wonder what a retrospective of my life would look like – how would my first 40 years look spread out on a canvas, whether captured through photographs or in a written sequence of marked moments?

At first glance I was hesitant to push forward as it seemed not only a monumental task, but also a bit self-aggrandizing. Why would anyone care about the musings of one individual's definitive life moments – especially if they aren't a celebrity or someone of consequence? However, when you consider *in part* what social media really is, then perhaps if the message were to be crafted the right way I could unfurl a collection of life moments and spread the *'love'* around a little bit and actually have it mean something.

Well, as the days dwindled and the birthday neared I oscillated back and forth on what this small endeavor might just look like. How would I capture the moments I felt were worthy enough of being shared with people who "kind of" know me and may even be interested in learning a bit more? For many of my social-media friends I had witnessed embracing this undertaking before me, the task-order seemed fairly clear. Pick a start date roughly 40 days out from said birthday and then let your life unfold in the order you see fit. As my first day approached I came close on more than one occasion to abandoning the notion altogether. It seemed more and more that I was setting myself up for embarrassment and failure. What happens when I just get plain tired of it all soon after I get started? What if my life just flat out isn't interesting? What if I failed? But rather than give in to the negative narrative on repeat in my head, I took a leap of faith - in myself.

I sat down on my starting day July 1, 2013 and said, *go*, - 40 days to glory. With one keystroke I began to type what would become a series of letters that drove me so far back into the mental rolodex of my life that I not only surprised myself but even seemed to rejuvenate the memories of several family members and friends who read them along the way. It was a journey, a walk back in time that brought a flood of tears, robust laughter, and even a few notes of gratitude; but most importantly it brought me closer to the person I had lost so many years before. I began to see me. I discovered in this collection of letters a human being who was worth more than the value I had placed upon him. I became a better father, a better son, a better friend and man by providing myself the gift of self-love and reflection that I had ignored for far too long.

While this was not at all the aim on Day One of the journey it soon became an exercise that I could only let unfold as if it were as natural as breathing itself. It became my meditative state of self-(*re*)discovery - to simply allow my mind to channel my past, recalling pieces of my life so emotionally tied to my present circumstance that it would uncover old wounds and begin a healing I could have only hoped for from previously discarded professional therapy sessions. I talked honestly for the first time in years. I spoke to myself with truth through the two most precious individuals in my life – my children, for they gave me new life through offering them the story of my own.

And so it began...

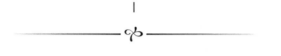

First and Fore(ty) most

40 days, 40 years, 40 life lessons –

WITH A NOD to David Stewart and Rodney Hobbs for inspiring the idea, I want to put a little spin on their creativity toward approaching the ripe old age of 40. As I head down the home stretch I would like to look back on 39 years and 325 days to recall a few life lessons that may or may *not* have an impact on the lives of my children in a somewhat comedic and not to be taken too seriously segment entitled, "Dear Basil and Sabine."

Day 1

Dear Basil and Sabine,

During my senior year of high school I decided to throw a party at Grandmama and Grandpa's house while they were out of town. At the time of conception it seemed like a really good idea, one that I could easily execute without harm to anyone, namely me. Simply disregard everything my Mom and Dad said about not having people in their house and make sure nothing of value breaks or looks out of place by the time they get back home. Easy like Sunday morning.

This party was going to ratchet up my cool points by a large margin as far as I was concerned. My plan was sure fire. I spread the word as best I could in those pre-internet days and hoped for the maximum in return. On the day of the party I had a keg of beer delivered to the house, the pool was clean and I made sure to remove all of the 'breakable' items from plain sight. I was ready and had all my bases covered. Well, by the time the party got really going, cars were parked down the length of the street. Beware the power of word of mouth. For a while everything seemed to be going pretty much as I had planned until one friend who shall remain nameless found Grandmama's Appleton Jamaican Rum inside of a downstairs liquor cabinet. She *really* seemed to enjoy the taste -- so much so she got pretty sick and Daddy got scared. I had to spend much of that night and the next day making sure she was OK while the party went on without any real governance.

When I finally got everyone safely out of the party I began the gargantuan task of cleaning my parent's house as best I could from top to bottom. There were absolutely no cool points to be found as I scrubbed, mopped, and wiped up things I had no business seeing in a house *or pool*, let alone one that belonged to George and Linda Mann. I cleaned every square inch of mess I could find, both inside and out, making sure I left no stone unturned in my attempt to leave the house spotless; returning all pertinent items to their rightful place. By the time my parents arrived back home I was sure of my victory. But guess who was smarter than Daddy was? -- Yup, Grandmama and Grandpa.

MORAL - No teenager on earth will have their parents' house looking and smelling better than what it was before they left unless something went terribly wrong.

40 days, 40 years, 40 life lessons - Day 2

Dear Basil and Sabine,

OK, this story is going to require a bit of background. As you get older you will hear people say, 'it takes a village...' (*You'll understand, let me explain*). Growing up my church family belonged to Bethel Missionary Baptist Church, Rev. Dr. Edward L. Hunt, Pastor of Wappinger Falls, NY. Choir rehearsal was Thursday night; Sunday school began at 9:30am, Devotion at 10:30am, and morning worship began at 11am - industry standard for the black church-going contingent.

Now, Deaconess Ruth Galloway was my Sunday school teacher, she was also the neighborhood seamstress. Mrs. Galloway ruled her Sunday school class by waving a long silver antenna with a dexterity that would have made Zorro jealous. Mrs. Campbell, another Sunday school teacher of mine was also the church pianist; additionally she would provide private piano lessons to children at her home during the week. Daddy spent a "very pleasant" half-hour with Mrs. Campbell for many a Wednesday evening going over the scales. And then there was Mrs. Myrick, our youth choir director who had a doctorate in giving the "STARE" (*similar to the one you see Daddy working on*). She had it perfected and could freeze everyone from the sopranos, three rows back to the tenors and bass.

Now you see, I tell you all of this because each of these women that were part of the village, would get their hair done down in Grandmama's basement every week. Yup, your Grandmama was also the neighborhood beautician. Week after week, I would see each of these women not just at church, but my house and just about everywhere else it seemed. So suffice it to say, Grandmama had eyes everywhere. There was no escape. So it was best to behave when you left the front door.

Well, one day as a member of the youth choir Daddy was selected to have his first solo. It was sort of a rite of passage in the church. I was so nervous. You want me to sing in front of everyone in church? - Yikes! Daddy was given the song, 'Witness for My Lord' and the choir practiced once a week at rehearsal right up until it was Second Sunday (Youth Sunday). I sat in the choir stand that Sunday alongside the other tenors anxiously awaiting my solo until finally the moment in the service arrived for the choir selection. Mrs. Myrick stood from her front row seat in the choir stand, turned and lifted her hands signaling for us to rise and then *looked* at me to come forward from my seat. I took my place behind the microphone, trying hard not to look out into the congregation as I lowered the mic stand to meet my height. With my hands shaking a little bit, Mrs. Campbell started to play the piano, I looked down at her and she nodded back up to me. I looked over at Mrs. Myrick, she *looked* right back at me and then off I went..., *"Is there anybody here who will testifyyyy..."* Uh oh, what was that? Something is happening. Wouldn't you know it, right in the middle of those first few precious notes, Daddy's voice decided to make a drastic change on him. I was so off-key I could hear the faint sound of dogs barking off in the distance. I froze in fear. But Mrs. Campbell kept playing, so Daddy kept going, even though I could tell my fellow choir members were behind me giggling. I was shrinking in embarrassment as I stood there afraid to look out into the congregation. However as the music played, the words continued coming out of my mouth. Then, just as I was about to start the next verse of the solo and despite my varied, vocal toned crooning, and nervousness, I looked up from the floor and out into the congregation and focused on the biggest smile looking right back at me. Mrs. Galloway was sitting there rocking slowly and nodding her head in appreciation. So I just kept singing. And then I looked and saw Mrs. Pat Knight out there smiling broadly as she was known for; Mrs. Doris Pleasants was smiling and rocking side to side, so again I looked down at the piano and Mrs. Campbell just kept playing. Mrs. Myrick, well she just kept the choir on time for the harmony and I kept on singing the whole song. I believe I may have even heard hands clapping at the end.

You know what girls, if I could have a wish today -- I would go back to Bethel and ask if I could sing that solo again. And I would want Mrs. Galloway sitting right there where she was, Mrs. Campbell right back at the piano and Mrs. Myrick *looking* right back in my direction.

MORAL - Sing out loud girls, not only does God smile, but so do the ladies in church.

40 days, 40 years, 40 life lessons - Day 3

Dear Basil and Sabine,

FAMILY - Now this is simple and difficult all at the same time. I wish I could say I have a clear-cut answer for you or that there was one set definition to family; there isn't. Family takes on different shapes, sizes, forms, and intense, heated battles over card games. What I am going to try and do is give you my true feelings on the value and importance of family. Your father grew up in a household filled with a great deal of **love**. Grandmama and Grandpa made sure that cousins Nene, Carolyn, Uncle Dwayne, and I didn't want for anything and understood what it meant to be respectful of one another as a family. Our traditions were similar to what you might see in other families: dinner around 6pm, big Sunday breakfast, summer vacation to the beach, plentiful Thanksgiving dinners, Christmas around the tree, and incredible birthdays - all spent with family.

As you two get older you are going to begin to see a larger picture surrounding some of the complexities of family and you will start to form your own opinions based on your life experiences. Your Grandpa is known to say when traveling to see loved ones, 'after 3 days fish and family start to smell the same' (*you'll understand that around your college years*) - What I need you to understand is that Family is to be valued and appreciated, bottom line. Your cousins, aunts, uncles, parents, and grandparents love you. We will be here for you when you need us and even when you think you don't need us -- we will be there too! Now here's the rub, family is going to disappoint you, family is going to frustrate the $#*t out of you, and sadly, sometimes family may decide to leave you. But girls, trust Daddy when I say this, *your* family will always **love** you and stand by you. Your mommy and daddy will go to the ends of the earth for you. As will your grandparents, your uncles Bakari and Dwayne, cousins Nene and Carolyn, and too many other family members to name.

Now, a lesson your father learned far too late in life is that you can't keep turning away from family and expect family to not feel neglected and devalued. If you truly want the love and respect of the family you claim to love, then it is upon you to nurture, value, and respect that family. Never should you expect your family, or friends you consider family for that matter, to waste a lifetime waiting for you to get your act together. Life is too short and this weather is scaring the $#*t out of some of us. (Save the polar bears!)

Basil and Sabine, I want you to always remember that as sisters you both are the best friends each of you will have in life. I need you to understand that and carry your love for one another oh so very close as you grow older. This is your family and this is where the love begins.

When Daddy drives us all up to Grandmama & Grandpa's house in upstate New York you may wonder why I do it in the dead of night as you both sleep. It's not because I don't want to have stimulating conversation with you in the car. It's because I want to get home to family the quickest way possible.

MORAL – Watch the final scene to the movie Claudine, it's a good definition of family. (And as Gladys Knight and the Pips said, *Make Yours a Happy Home*)

40 days, 40 years, 40 life lessons - Day 4

Dear Basil and Sabine,

When I was in the 7th grade I shared several classes with a boy named Kareem 'Monty' Montague. I immediately immaturely passed judgment on Kareem. I didn't understand him and here's why: Kareem was smart, smarter than I could comprehend. He excelled in most anything he put his heart and mind to. In Latin he was the Homer of verb conjugation; in Mrs. Habib's 8th period math class he once presented her with a mathematical algorithm so obscure, all she could do was nod assuredly and stare at him in disbelief. While Daddy sat in 8th chair alto saxophone, guess who he had to look at sitting over in first chair trumpet? That's right, Kareem.

From 7th to 12th grade Daddy could not figure Kareem out. And I realize now so clearly why -- While your father was so busy trying to be accepted by his classmates and make them laugh, Kareem was focused on success. While Daddy was too lazy to pay attention to homework, Kareem was focused on the next level. When Daddy felt it was cooler to horse around in school rather than pay closer attention to the Kareem model, Kareem was being accepted to Harvard.

And off he went after high school graduation to wear the Crimson. Like many people after high school, Kareem and I lost touch with one another. But an invention came along called Facebook and it has an interesting way of pulling people back together with one another from years past. It turns out that young boy Kareem from daddy's 7th grade math class is now Lieutenant Colonel Kareem Montague of the Army's 82nd Airborne. He has served his country proudly with honor and dignity, commanding some of the bravest men and women in our nation's military on the field of battle.

As a Lieutenant in the United States Navy when daddy has the honor to confront Kareem, I will come to attention and salute this higher-ranking officer and render him the respect he has so rightfully earned. And I will do it with a great sense of pride and humility; knowing that his model is one of which I want you both to look to as an example of what the value of intelligence is. There is nothing wrong with being smart. There is nothing wrong with the pursuit of knowledge. Seek it, Treasure it, and pack as much of it away as possible. And have **no fear** of education and the success it will bring your way.

MORAL – Careful of passing judgment along life's path, because you just may have to confront your Kareem one day.

⁊

40 days, 40 years, 40 life lessons –
Day 5

Dear Basil and Sabine,

Your Uncle Dwayne and I were talking not long ago about life and some of the choices we have both made over the years. In the midst of the conversation when I was feeling particularly perplexed by some of my own decisions your uncle said something that although didn't seem quite prophetic at the time -- it keeps playing over and over in my head. He said, "…it all comes from somewhere."

(*Now bear with me here…*)

As children, the 3 of us, Dwayne, Carolyn and your father shared a fairly fruitful childhood filled with all manner of youthful experiences – I could probably write you an encyclopedia (*these don't exist anymore btw*) on how I tormented each of them. Somewhere around the early to mid-1980s your grandparents brought home this thing called a VCR (*these may still exist*). You could watch movies with this thing right in your own home. Now, on the main thoroughfare (Route 9) that ran through the town where daddy grew up there was a store called Sound Odyssey. They essentially sold stereo equipment, but when VCRs started to pop up in houses, they began to rent VCR tapes. They easily had 1,000 movies to choose from.

Now every Friday Grandpa would take the three of us into Sound Odyssey so we each could pick out a movie to watch. The usual breakdown went something like this, Daddy would get some action-thriller movie, Carolyn would get something I didn't understand, often with sub-titles, and Uncle Dwayne would get a musical. I mean week after week after week, your uncle would have a continuous cycle of musicals on repeat – Annie, Grease, Dreamgirls, and Chitty-Chitty Bang Bang!! They were *killing* me! "Doesn't anyone want to watch Terminator with me?!?!

In a selfish rush I'd watch my movie first, typically by myself and then go outside and play the rest of the weekend. But if it ever rained, oh man Daddy was doomed, I would be stuck inside listening to, "The sun'll come out tomorrow, bet your bottom dollar that tomorrowwwww, there'll be sun…" It was non-stop with your uncle. But you know something girls; it's funny, today at almost 40 years old I can sing you songs from all of those movies Uncle Dwayne brought home, but I barely remember anything relevant about the movies I would get. So if you are ever wondering why Daddy recently bought the blu-ray DVD of Chitty-Chitty Bang Bang or why I may spontaneously break out and start singing, "STEPPIN' TO THE BAD SIDE, OOOHHH, OOHHH, OOOHHH, GONNA TAKE A MEAN RIDE, OOOOHHH, OOOOHH, OOOHHH…" Well, it all comes from somewhere.

MORAL – Make sure the good things stick.

✂

40 days, 40 years, 40 life lessons – Day 6

Dear Basil and Sabine,

This letter is actually more of an observation than it is a lesson for you to adhere to. At least right now it is. You have often heard me talk about growing up in Wappinger Falls and as little girls you would ask me many, many questions about Grandmama and Grandpa's house when we came to visit. While most things in and around their house look relatively the same, there are a few subtle changes that have taken place over time. That's just a part of life.

Today, you are uber-excited when we travel north as you get to visit the neighbors across the street at 6 Deer Run. John and Judy along with their children welcome you into their yard while you help Owen, Eileen, and Brian bring just about every toy imaginable out into the driveway. And while you are doing that I undoubtedly bore their father John to death with stories of how I used to play in that very yard growing up. And when I say *play*, oh man, the kids on my block were in that yard from sun up to sun down. The family that lived there back then had three daughters and their father was the person who taught daddy how to play croquet. I think Mr. Danek got tired of seeing the kids destroy his lawn playing kickball and wanted to show us a little civilization.

As I look back and think of the families that lived on that block I realize something quite valuable. There were the Chen's (Alice, Eric); the Naik's (Manish, Rupal); the Danek's (Gabrielle, Kristina, and Angelique); the Mann's (Carolyn, Bashon, and Dwayne); the Shah's (Nirav); and the Hsi's (James, Kevin, Brian). It was a block so culturally diverse we could have called ourselves the United Nations. And at no point while growing up did that at all seem odd, wrong, or out of place. We ate together, played together, grew up together, and whether we knew it or not, I believe we challenged each other. Now I am going to need a little help remembering and maybe I will ask one of my old neighbors if and when I see them again, but I think collectively between those children our college choices looked something like this: MIT, Harvard, Cornell, UNC-Chapel Hill, RPI, Johns Hopkins, UVa, and NYU. I may have missed a couple. Nevertheless, I believe there was something in the water on the street we grew up on.

Girls, diversity is a good thing, a **GREAT** thing in fact. Surround yourself with good people diverse in ethnicity, diverse in thought, and diverse in socio-economic makeup. You will be the better for it.

MORAL – You are who you hang around.

40 days, 40 years, 40 life lessons –
Day 7

Dear Basil and Sabine,

I am not sure yet how I will eventually present this collection of letters to you, but if I could ask you each to read one letter before all of the others it is this one. If for no other reason than that it reflects a great deal of the meaning behind why I am doing this in the first place.

In horse racing there is a term used for a horse that doesn't make it to the gate, it is referred to as a DNP – Did Not Post. The horse, for whatever reason couldn't run the race. I have seen several times where a horse can be heavily favored to run well in a high stakes race and then at the very last second the trainer will pull them out. It reminds me of something I learned in Mr. Sonntag's Physics class. Whole lotta' potential energy, no kinetic energy (unbelievable, that was Daddy remembering something from high school physics!) So you are now asking yourself what horse racing and physics have to do with you?! (*Apologies, daddy is long-winded and takes a while to get to the point.*)

Words and actions are a lot like potential and kinetic energy. They both have power and can have a considerably measurable effect based on the context within which they are used or executed. Over the years I have found that while spoken or written words can be a nice thing, they can also be an empty thing. There is a deliverable beyond the words based on the premise of one's actions that can determine the worth or sense of value associated with the words in the first place. My actions as your father have to play a greater role in your life such that whatever I may write to you within these letters or say to you as you grow older is thereby reinforced and given greater perspective. Far too many times in my own life I used the gift of elocution to create potential energy, only to under deliver on the kinetic. Over time people catch on to that faulty defect and no matter what you say or how you deliver your words again, they will ultimately fall on deaf ears.

With this letter Daddy is really writing to himself girls -- a reminder that as I look back along the path of my life there are far too many instances of empty words with minimal sequential action. Or, action that detracted from the words spoken in the first place. Understand this is not so much regret, but more so an opportunity to minimize any further DNP in my life.

MORAL – If you say you will run the race - just like Secretariat in the Belmont, get out front early and run **your** race.

⚯

40 days, 40 years, 40 life lessons –
Day 8

Dear Basil and Sabine,

There is a magical place in the Hudson Valley where children laughed, played, and lived out dreams while parents rushed from work, cheered, and wiped away tears strewn from elbow scrapes, raspberries and little league heartbreak. That place was Robinson Lane. I'm smiling just saying the name. From T-ball to Big Boy, Robinson Lane was my Field of Dreams before I ever knew who Kevin Costner was or where Iowa stood on a map. From March to June it was a little slice of heaven on earth.

From the age of 9 to 12 years old Daddy played on a little league baseball team by the name of Rowe Rutledge. Our colors were pine tree green and delicious apple red. Girls, it felt so good to put on that uniform and run out there on that field. Daddy would chew this shredded bubble gum called Big League Chew and act like I was Reggie Jackson (Google him). On those teams daddy had teammates like Kevin and Devin Travis, Scott Neave, Jason Vitale, Kevin Baird, Derick Santis, Jason Kowalski, Ken Christman, Kieran Lalor, little Ned, and quiet Geoff. One of the best parts of being on that team though was our cheering section. The Rowe Rutledge Rowdies were what they came to be known as. They never saw a whistle they didn't like to blow!

This "special" crew of parents and supporters were rock solid. The leader was Kevin and Devin's mom, Mrs. Travis. She could single-hand-edly out scream all the moms and dads from the opposing team. But she also had one hell of a support staff. You see Mrs. Travis would bring her other children to all of our games. Deborah, Sonora and little baby Alan. They would all arrive in their father's chocolate brown Lincoln Continental. I swear Mr. Travis was smooth like glass when he rolled down Robinson in that car, his left hand waving to folks and that broad smile you could see from a baseball field away. And for six innings on a Tuesday night, Saturday morning, or Sunday afternoon the Travis family and the rest of the 'Rowdies' would cheer us on. They cheered us all the way to a little league championship.

There are going to be times in your life girls that in the moment you won't think about twice, but over time you will want to go back to those spaces and places in time and hold onto them forever -- wishing perhaps you could just catch a familiar smell to cherish and recollect. Mr. and Mrs. Travis are no longer with us now and I know they watch over their lovely children from heaven, whether an Iowa cornfield or Robinson Lane. In my little slice of heaven I can see that whole Travis family and all those other parents leading the familiar chant, Go Rowe Rutledge!!

MORAL – Pay attention to your loudest cheering section, they'll get you through it all.

૪

40 days, 40 years, 40 life lessons
Day 9

Dear Basil and Sabine,

There are some lessons in life that will take you several years, maybe even decades to fully comprehend. I hope the value of saving money is something you understand fairly early in your life. But, there is also the lesson of personal sacrifice that tends to go hand in hand with the first one.

From a very young age I was impressed by **new** things. There used to be a popular brand of jeans called *Sergio Valente*, they had these two stylish V's on the back pockets that I was particularly impressed with. Daddy couldn't wait to get his skinny behind into a pair of those bad boys. I convinced Grandpa to pay me a dollar for every home run I hit in Little League and at the end of the baseball season I had 18 smackeroos to play with. Well, Mr. Valente charged about $30 for his jeans. Daddy had to go in hock to his parents because I just had to have that denim on me. This trend continued as I grew older - parachute pants, bomber jacket, MJ Thriller jacket, first ever pair of Air Jordan's, Troop jacket, nameplate chain, etc. If it was the latest fashion trend, I needed it and would spend my money and even more of Grandmama and Grandpa's money to get it.

What Daddy never took time to notice however, was while I was wearing all of the latest styles and getting a brand new Honda XR-80 dirt bike for Christmas of '84 - is how much hard work, savings and sacrifice was going on somewhere else in order for all these gifts and opportunities to actually appear. I mean Grandmama just does hair on nights and weekends after her day job as a Principal because she likes it right? Grandpa plows driveways in the winter and works for that polyurethane company in the Bronx in addition to being a Guidance Counselor because it's a cool thing to do right? I guess they both just like buying used cars because new cars have a funny smell. Nope, wrong answer.

Your grandparents did what they had to do so the children under their roof could have every experience they wanted for them. They made sure 4 children had brand name clothes to go to school in; took family vacations to Cape Cod, Lake George and Virginia Beach regularly; skied everywhere from Jiminy Peak, Mass. to Okemo, VT and even drove in a '74 Ford F-250 with a camper hitched to the back all the way to Disney World. And after all of that would you believe Daddy had the onions to complain to Grandmama why we didn't have wall to wall carpet like the other families I knew. Girls, I am actually very lucky to still have a head on my shoulders after that one. I didn't appreciate their sacrifice. I didn't see what was happening so clearly in front of me. They saved and they went without some of the finer things so their children could be happy.

Today, so many years later, Daddy still struggles with not wanting to buy shiny new things or even gaining an appreciation for the art of saving for a rainy day. I do know that both of you girls deserve every opportunity and more to enjoy life and grow; same as I received from my parents growing up, so perhaps that notion should propel my learning curve a bit more rapidly. I could write you 100 letters about the perils of money and the ridiculous things I have wasted money on over the years, but for now I want you to focus on what is truly important here - to appreciate what someone else gives up so that you can have your Sergio's in life.

MORAL – You don't need to win a Superbowl to get to Disney World, just a happy family, an old Ford, and a savings account.

⚘

40 days, 40 years, 40 life lessons - Day 10

Dear Basil and Sabine,

At six and four years of age you are both still new to the ultimate **joy** of "snow days". When I was just a bit older than you are now the very hint of a possible snow day would elicit an unbridled display of excitement. It would have me gazing out of my bedroom window at night, nose pressed firmly against the cold glass casting my eyes to the skies above, waiting ever so patiently for the first flake to fall. It is an intricate ritual most any school age child can appreciate - and some adults for that matter. I remember many an early snowy morning listening to updates on K104-FM, waiting for them to announce that familiar phrase..."Wappinger Central School District - 2 hour delay, no morning Kindergarten" or the Grand Poohbah announcement, "Wappinger Central School District - CLOSED." *Cue the music... *"DANCIN', DANCIN', DANCINNNN'...I'm a DANCIN' MACHINEEEEE"* -- And I would dance my way all the way down the hallway toward the kitchen and then **Bammm!** There it was, "The List."

You see, for some reason Poughkeepsie City School District never caught on to the school cancellation act. They would send their kids to school even if a glacier fell on Dutchess County. And, since Grandmama worked in PCSD she would have to leave the house early and her children were left to hang out all day. Soooo, sleep in until noon and play out in the snow right?!?!? Wrong, no chance, Do Not Pass Go, Do Not Collect $200, go directly to the broom closet and start cleaning the house. In bright yellow legal pad paper (*She loved this stuff*) Grandmama would leave us a 'list' of things to do before she got home. Even today, you can look at the trim next to the doorway of the kitchen and see all of the old tack marks from where her lists would reside. It's on the right side of the doorway and got higher as we got older. And don't even think about not doing one of the listed items; there would be a price to pay if something wasn't done. So off we would go to attack the 'list'.

Well girls, here is what I would like to do. Since you live in Washington D.C. and get snow days whenever they call for snow in Illinois, I am going to approach the legacy of the 'list' in a slightly different fashion. Every 10th letter I write to you is going to consist of a list of things. Things I want for you, things I want you to consider, places I want you to go, maybe even specific movies you should be sure to watch in your lifetime. Just a sample of random thoughts really -- please find your first List below:

10 Things you will do or know how to do before you turn 18:

1. You will know how to change a tire
2. You will know how to change the oil on a car
3. You will know how to bait a hook
4. You will know how to drive a stick shift
5. You will know how to get places without using GPS
6. You will be familiar with seamanship (read: boat handling)
7. You will be prepared for college
8. You will understand the danger of credit cards
9. You will have had a job, or 2, or 3
10. You will graduate high school on time or sooner

*BONUS - You *might* have an iPhone

(And Grandmama didn't ruin snow days; we still got out and enjoyed the fun. She just reinforced the notion that sitting around doing nothing all day is not acceptable when you aren't paying rent!)

MORAL - Make a list, write things down, this way you won't forget ANYTHING.

ℚ

40 days, 40 years, 40 life lessons – Day 11

Dear Basil and Sabine,

As you know, children can have a lot of allergies as they grow up. Shellfish, peanut butter, pollen; if you aren't careful and get a hold of the wrong thing it can make you quite uncomfortable. Well when Daddy was younger he was allergic to homework and the National Honor Society. I had a strong belief that if I got too close I might just break out and start scratching uncontrollably. I knew just how far I had to stay away in order to be safe. One of the reasons why that was just a ridiculous and lazy notion on my part is that I had some great teachers along the way that really took the time to push me forward and ask more of me than I was willing to give. This is part of what makes teachers so special.

Teachers are going to exist throughout your life. This is a good thing. There will be classroom teachers from nursery school through your college years and there will also be those teachers who you will be fortunate enough to encounter as you walk your life's path, whose words and presence will help you evolve and mature as a person. I would like to use this letter so that I might share with you a few memories from the teachers throughout my life. I'll have you know that their influence has been integral to some of the smallest details of my being; they have also provided some of the strictest regimens and philosophies of thought that I carry with me today.

Here it goes - I went to Hull Homestead Nursery School run by Judy and her husband John where I had my first introduction to true organic living (I mean they had a real tee-pee on the property). My Kindergarten teacher Mrs. Garish and her assistant Ms. Thomas at Fishkill Plains assured me that finger painting is not only safe, it's encouraged at nearly any age. Vassar Road Elementary School: 1st grade – Mrs. Nichols may you rest in peace ma'am, with your smile and compassion, you touched us all. 2nd grade – Mrs. Pelton, who would always blow her nose and keep the tissue in the sleeve of her sweater; sweetest lady ever, but it was difficult to watch that tissue go back up the sleeve every day. 3rd grade – Mrs. Synette, she made multiplication fun, best smiley faces on the top of your quiz EVER (seriously, they winked at you). 4th grade - Mr. Miles, well, he just made 4th grade cool (had a mustache only rivaled by Magnum P.I.). 6th grade – Enter Mr. Don Chisamore, he kept his class in line by having blank spaces on the black board every morning that looked like this _ _ _ _ _ _ _ _. If we got too loud over the course of the day it would look like this: NO RECESS.

By the time I got to Van Wyck Jr. High I had several teachers over the course of a single day. Mr. Roberts in Latin once got really upset that every student purposefully left their text books in our lockers as a practical joke so he gave us a one-question test on the name of the text book publisher -- Touché Magister, touché. In Mrs. Hirschmann's 6th period English class we once sat and watched a very sad Space Shuttle launch where another teacher and her fellow astronauts perished after liftoff. At John Jay High School Mr. Knickerbocker is the reason daddy can type without looking down at the keyboard; Mr. Eidle, Sir may I say gratias tibi ago; ego erubisco tu and may you too rest in peace. We should have treated you better. That spitball to the chest was (*to quote Charles Barkley*)... 'TURRIBLE!' Thank you Mr. Archimede for drilling me on solving for x and discovering the word hypotenuse, (I've never used it in a sentence until now, but I might name a pet after it.) Ms. Zimmerman, you made Chemistry interesting to say the least, but I'll be honest with you I would take those NYC kids out for a steak dinner that "borrowed" the Regents exam back in '89 and then shared it with the *New York Daily News*. Mr. Green, thank you for channeling my love of sports and incorporating it into my writing, somewhere there exists a miniature screenplay written by yours truly and produced by Mike Mostransky starring Jeremy Pond and William Monden that could possibly deserve a shot at a 30 for 30 (*it's a classic*). And to Mrs. Barbara Searle who instilled a passion for English prose and Mrs. McCabe for making me focus on the freedom of IMPROV, I truly profess a humble 'Thank You' (My present and past tense use is all over the place, but I'm able to pay a mortgage now).

These teachers and several others left an indelible mark on daddy growing up. I have a great amount of respect for their ability to reach children of all ages to not only mentor and learn, but to aspire and achieve more than just settling for being average. You will have *great* teachers in your lives girls, and you may not even truly realize their impact until well after you have left their classroom. Relish the fact that their lessons will hold firm and true so long as your willingness to listen and learn stays forever a priority, no matter how old you are.

MORAL – Keep being two of the best teacher's daddy has ever had ok? I like coming to class.

40 days, 40 years, 40 life lessons – Day 12

Dear Basil and Sabine,

I want you to know that these letters are meant to be used merely as a guide throughout your life, nothing more, maybe a little less. With God's blessing you will undoubtedly both grow up to be beautiful, smart women with a mind of your own who have the acute ability to make smart, sound decisions based on deductive reasoning. And please know that your father is admittedly still trying to navigate his own life while making better choices and thinking more about the consequences of his own actions. But there are some decisions in life you have to make early and stick to your guns no matter what the end results may be.

Now what I am about to tell you is very important to me and though there are other people who will **strongly** disagree, (*Grandpa being one of them*) you are just going to have to understand that in this country people are free to life, liberty, and the pursuit of being a fan of whatever sports team they wish. There are some who have NO choice in the matter and others who just choose wrong. But in *this* house, we root for the following: The New York Yankees, The New York Knicks, and The New York Football Giants, (*the Jets and Mets hold a place in the guest room*), and while **hate** is a word I do not wish for you to use in your vocabulary, Daddy is telling you right now that it is ok to have a tempered distaste for the Boston Red Sox, the Baltimore Orioles, the Indiana Pacers, the Miami Heat, and the rest of the NFC east.

Now let's start with Grandpa, because this is worth explaining and needs your attention. As you get older you will understand more clearly the legacy of Jackie Robinson and the Brooklyn Dodgers and what it meant not only to baseball but also to the discussion and evolution of race and equality in America. It's a topic I cannot fully convey in one letter to you. But we *will* be discussing this many, many times down the road. Now your grandpa is a lifelong Jackie Robinson fan and I have nothing but the deepest respect and admiration for his affinity. It is a respect not only for a baseball player, but for the courage of a man standing up for principle in the face of great human indecency. And Jackie Robinson played for the Dodgers of Brooklyn, New York in the National League, as did one Willie Mays of the New York Baseball Giants. Between Ebbets Field and the Polo Grounds, this was grandpa's slice of heaven on earth.

Now when it came time for Daddy to play Little League and they asked which league I would be trying out for, Grandpa stepped in and said the National League. And if you ask him, he will gladly tell you why he wanted this for me. But here's what happened along the way to Cooperstown girls. When it came time for Grandpa to take Daddy to his first baseball game, he brought me to a mystical place in the Bronx, New York called Yankee Stadium and on that green, lush field was number 44, Reggie Jackson. Game over. Oh Grandpa would eventually take me to Shea Stadium soon after and I remember quite clearly sitting there with Grandpa, Grandmama and Mr. and Mrs. George Wyatt, Grandpa's god-parents. I even remember the New York Metropolitans holding flip-flop day at the ball-park; after a bad call by an umpire nearly every flip-flop landed on the field to the raucous chant of "FLIP-FLOP, FLIP-FLOP!!!" There were also chance meetings with Darryl Strawberry and Dwight Gooden (*2 unfortunate stories*) outside of the player's entrance to Shea Stadium that couldn't turn me around. I was a Yankee fan.

Everything else just sort of slid into place. My first trip to Madison Square Garden was to see Bernard King and the Knickerbockers take on

Dr. Julius Irving and the Philadelphia 76ers. Six year old Bashon Mann was going to be that tall one day, I just knew it. I was a Knicks fan.

Football is slightly more confusing, but just know that Grandmama loved her some Broadway Joe Namath, so the Jets were beloved, but the Giants eventually ruled out when Lawrence Taylor and Bill Parcells came to town. I admit to abandoning the Giants for a brief time after an unfortunate run-in with linebacker Carl Banks during an 8th grade field trip to the Statue of Liberty – all you had to do was sign the piece of paper Carl. But things with the Jets went sour over time, especially when things got a little weird with their coach involving toes, tattoos, and their quarterback situation, so I kind of pulled myself away. It just made me feel a little yucky inside.

Now I understand you both were born in Washington D.C., and daddy has already taken you to several Washington Nationals games so perhaps I may have already tainted the water just a little bit (though we spend more time on their playground than actually watching the game). There is a General Manager for the Washington Basketball team, Les Bullets that Daddy has a personal problem with stemming back to his days in New York and he continues to show his ineptitude for the business year after year, so we won't be cheering them on either anytime soon. The local pigskin team is a complete soap opera and is merely here for entertainment purposes *off* the field, and due to the whole NFC East rule I laid out earlier I simply watch that side show as an idle bystander.

Ladies, let the record show, I have **clearly** laid out my agenda for you here and should you wish for a lifetime of enjoyment while following sports, you would be doing yourselves a favor by adhering to the **strong advice** as laid out above. It's some of the best I can give you.

MORAL – that extra place I leave at the dinner table is for Numbah 2 Derek Jeter, Numbah 2...

℘

40 days, 40 years, 40 life lessons – Day 13*

Dear Basil and Sabine,

There are going to be days when I don't have an answer to that question you ask. 99 times out of 100 when you ask me questions I am usually able to reply quite promptly with a satisfactory response or at least provide you with a witty retort that will stump you for a few seconds. But from last night thru this morning I can't give you the answer for the question floating through my own head -- a question of how can I protect you from evil and injustice in the world. I wish that weren't so, but even parents will be at a loss for words from time to time. There are going to be things in life that leave us dismayed no matter how old we are. In these times I find it is best to sit still in a quiet place and lean on **your** higher power for strength and understanding. After watching the news last night I went into your room while you were sleeping with your new dolls and kissed you both. That was my answer to the sadness and anger consuming me, and today I will hug and kiss you more. You will have more letters to read girls, but today I want you to know that I love you and pray evil never comes in your direction.

MORAL – Your hugs mean just as much to me as they do to you.
   (***Night of the Trayvon Martin verdict announcement***)

40 days, 40 years, 40 life lessons – Day 14

Dear Basil and Sabine,

When I began this small letter campaign I had a loose plan to walk you sequentially through my life and provide you small tidbits from a few adventures along the way. However, I continue to find that just as you may have plans to go in one direction, something occurs to show you just how little you actually are in control (**MESSAGE!!**). One day perhaps we can all sit down and discuss the past couple of days in greater depth, but yesterday was too significant for me to let another moment go by without capturing it for you. I am unsure of how clear your memories will be of the day and I don't want to forget it either so I am writing it down now for all of us.

I admit that Sunday, July 14th 2013 started off a bit melancholy and I am certain there were a few other people who felt the same. Our national conversation has shifted once again and there are new mountains to climb, more valleys to walk across. But we were blessed with a new day and there was life to live, so we did. Basil, we agreed earlier in the week that with Grandmama coming into town it would be a perfect time for you to conduct your swim test at the Joint Base Anacostia-Bolling swimming pool. You had it in your head that you could do it despite my persistent questioning, and you made sure everyone you came across knew what your intentions were – TO TAKE YOUR SWIM TEST. Well, Saturday was jam packed with an American Girl Store visit (Parents, I call foul on this BTW!) and birthday parties so we could not get to the pool. Sunday morning you insisted rain or shine there had better be a swim test on your agenda. Mother Nature heard you loud and clear; she pulled back the clouds and launched the mercury clear to 97. Houston, we are *go* for launch.

Now we have watched children older than you last summer and much of this one take that swim test with varying degrees of success. It is an Olympic size pool and you are required to swim the width back and forth and then tread water for 60 seconds in order to pass. It is not easy. I admit to wondering, quite aloud on occasion whether you were ready for this feat. By the time you jumped in the water yesterday I think you were ready to tell me where I could shove my 'doubting Thomas' attitude. You entered the pool slowly and just like that you took off -- Whoosh! You shot off the wall underwater and then came up with your version of freestyle and kept it going as I was following along nearly running face-first into the lifeguard tower and before I knew it you had made it to the other side. I could see on your face that you were clearly tired, but you took a few deep breaths and started your trek back. I could see now that you were laboring a little but you just kept those little legs kicking and arms scooping for that mint chocolate chip ice cream. By now everyone was looking your direction because your crazed father was shouting loud enough for much of the base to hear. The look of genuine determination on your face made me want to jump in that pool with you as you neared the wall and you know what Basil??? You Did It!!! You made it clear across the width of that pool... Twice!! I wanted to break dance! By the time daddy calmed down you were already 40 seconds into the treading water sequence as you simply let your body float on that water for what had to be a minute and change. No more red-band for you, green all summer!

When I finally had a moment to collect my thoughts of the day and think about the events that unfolded I was reminded of a movie daddy enjoyed when he was younger called Parenthood with Steve Martin, where he plays a father to 3 children. There is a scene in the movie where the Dad goes berserk over his son catching a fly ball to win a baseball game. Afterward the Dad was amazed at how such a small thing as catching a fly ball could mean so much in his own life. And yesterday I had **that** moment. It was so great for you and it meant so much for me to see you accomplish what you knew you were going to do all along, despite my worry and concern to the contrary. You never doubted yourself. You are 6 friggin' years old and you taught me something yesterday I have been trying to nail down for much of my life. You believed in yourself. You would think of all the times I listened to Lena Horne in the Wiz it would have sunk in by now (*musicals and your Uncle...*). Thank you Basil; for showing me in your own little way that despite opposition and tide, strength of will and perseverance proves triumphant in *all* things.

MORAL – Dory was right, "Just keep swimming, just keep swimming."

P.S. – Hey Sabine, don't think I didn't see you imitating your sister yesterday either. I quietly sat and watched you traverse back and forth the width of the pool in your swim floats all by yourself just to prove that you are not far behind.

❦

40 days, 40 years, 40 life lessons – Day 15

Dear Basil and Sabine,

Should God allow, one day the two of you will confront me and offer the following words, "Dad, can I borrow your car?" and as my bottom lip begins to quiver, I will immediately fall faint, clutching my keys in a death grip. OK, maybe I won't faint, but I will certainly pause for a few seconds to collect myself before giving you an answer and just handing over those coveted keys. I suspect my parents went through the same decision process when it came time for me to drive alone. However, I do remember there were a few strict rules in place for me to adhere to before leaving the house. Respect the car, respect the road, respect yourself, and respect the time I have given you to have the car home by. Keep those in mind and you are off to a good start.

But before you go doing your best Danica Patrick, let me provide you with a quick driving lesson or two before you ask to borrow the keys. When daddy was about 15 or 16 years old there was a neighbor of his who was just learning how to drive. I believe she had her learner's permit (*you get this before your license*). Well, the young woman was in her driveway with her parent's car and suddenly something went awfully wrong. Now, you would have to ask her directly as no one in the neighborhood dared broach the topic with her at the time, but I don't think she meant to drive that car through the garage door like that. And stop laughing because she could have really hurt herself that day. And daddy could be hurt if she ever hears about me telling you this story. But she turned out ok and believe it or not it turns out garage doors can be replaced.

OK, to be honest with you I just about laughed myself silly when I saw that garage door sitting on the roof of that Volvo like that. But you know what *is* even more funny girls, there is something out there called Karma – simply put, 'what goes around, comes around.' One day, daddy was in the driveway with his first car. It was a 1978 Fiat Spyder that Grandmama used to drive. Convertible, leather seats and a wood grain steering wheel – Classic! (*Grandmama likes the wind in her hair!*)

So I'm in the driveway, the garage door is up mind you and Grandpa is in the garage telling me to back it in. OK, ease up off the clutch and ease down on the gas -- simple right? Well that message got lost from my brain to my feet in a millisecond, because my toes heard, "Let go of the clutch immediately and **slam** on the gas!!!" HOLY MOTHER OF PEARL!!! That car went from the driveway to the back of the garage faster than you can say, Doc McStuffins! To this day I don't how or what stopped that car from going clear through the back wall of the garage. Up until right now I have never really admitted what happened that day. I would usually just laugh it off and say that I had everything under control, but that is so far from the truth. Ask Grandmama and Grandpa, I am sure they remember that day quite clearly.

Also, before you take the keys you are going to have to listen to what Mommy and Daddy tell you about the responsibility of driving a car that doesn't belong to you. It is either your mother's or your father's car. You don't make the payments, you don't pay insurance and you (*at least for now*) do not pay for the gas. Someone else does and you should respect their property. One day daddy asked Grandpa if he could take his brand new 1991 Volkswagen Jetta to see a friend of his in New Jersey. Grandpa graciously said yes, with one rule. "Do **not** go into the city!" And what do you think Daddy did? Yup, MY POSSE's ON BROADWAY!!! SUN ROOF OPEN SO I COULD FEEL THE WIND BLOW! Look at all the people; look at all the lights, hey, look at the oil light?! Why is that on? Well, that must be a glitch right, I mean it **is** a brand new car. Nothing could possibly be wrong; I'll just keep driving until that nice little light goes off. I wish I could tell you this story has a happy ending. It doesn't. I am not sure what hurt Grandpa worse girls, the fact that I seized the engine on his brand new car or that I disrespected him by not heeding his words. I really hurt him. You never know what burden you put on the people who love you when you disobey them or give them a reason to distrust you (*we will talk more about trust later on*).

Look, I know that there are going to be countless days and nights that I will not breathe a sigh of relief until I hear the car pull into the driveway with the two of you back home safe and sound. What you need to fully understand and respect is that driving is a privilege ladies. You **do not** have a right to drive. You have to earn it. We will spend countless hours practicing how to drive. You will be *encouraged* to learn how to drive responsibly. And, if you want your own brand new car, guess what? You will buy one. You, yes *you*, will buy one. Forget everything you see on any reruns of MTV's Sweet 16, because those people are from outer space.

MORAL – Pay attention to the lights in your car, they're trying to tell you something.

40 days, 40 years, 40 life lessons – Day 16

Dear Basil and Sabine,

There is a line from one of my favorite movies, "Finding Forrester" where William Forrester, played by Sean Connery makes reference to the 'gift of friendship'. While I have made mention already that both of you girls as sisters will be the best friends you will have in life, I would be remiss if I didn't call attention to the special people in your life who you will be fortunate enough to call a 'friend.' This could be someone you meet at 5 or someone you come across at 75. I don't claim to know what the text book definition of friend is, but I guess I could just as easily use a dictionary (*keep one of these handy*). What I do know is over the years I have been blessed with all manner of friends who have come in and out of my life. And I remember all of them. There are school friends, neighborhood friends, friends of the family, work friends, close friends, not-so-close friends, there is this thing today called Facebook friends. But of all the friends out there in the world, there is nothing quite like a **BEST FRIEND**.

For some people a best friend is a dog or some other type of animal. For others a best friend is an inanimate object. For daddy, I have had the good fortune to call several people *friend* throughout my life. There was Jen Ryan from way back in Kindergarten, there was Katie Barton from down the street; there was Joey Buchalter and Rick Stringham from elementary school; and there was Jeremy Pond from high school. Now there were certainly other really good friends that Daddy had, each one of them very special to me and I will always remember some of the great adventures we had growing up, but there were two people that came into my life who I continue to share a very special bond with to this day – Jason Conrad and William Monden.

I could talk to you girls for hours about the crazy things the three of us have done over the years and still not capture the essence of what it meant to have them in my life. When I first met Jason I was mad at him immediately because *he* was dating the cutest girl in school and daddy wasn't allowed to date. When I met Uncle Will for the first time I couldn't stand him because he was better at basketball than I was and his team kept beating us. Though once we all found ourselves at the same high school much of that silliness went away and best friends was the only thing left on the table. There were basketball games, football games, girlfriends, proms, skipped classes, stolen De La Soul tapes, parties, road trips, college separation, strained friendship, marriages, children, parental loss, growth, and reconnection. We have been through a lot together and we have been through a lot separately.

At times daddy was not always the 'best friend' he should have been to both Jason and Will over all of the years we have known each other. I have had phases in my life where my own selfishness led to distance and strain in our friendships. But life has a funny way of bringing you full circle to where you see things through a much clearer lens and realize the importance of certain people in your life. This is when you swallow your pride and ask your friends for forgiveness. You will find that there are some things that are hard to say to people when they are standing right in front of you and are sometimes better said through your own written words. My advice would be if words ever fail you in a face to face meeting, take a moment, collect your thoughts and write down what you feel. I wish I could do that for all of the friends in my life, not always asking forgiveness but sometimes just to say hello and check in on them. I would say to Jen Ryan, congratulations on your new baby, I wish you an abundance of joy and happiness with your growing family. I would say to Katie Barton, you are doing **great**, just keep smiling and we'll see you in the summer down on B dock. I would say to Joey Buchalter, thank you Joey for treating me like a member of the family. With every bagel I eat I think of you and yours. I would say to Varick Stringham, when do we break out the dirt bikes again blood brother?! I would say to Jeremy Pond, thank you for being a true friend from the beginning man and for sharing time with your father with me.

And as for Jason and Will, well I would pick up the phone, I would write an email and I would put you both in the car and travel right to their front door and say, "Thank you for being my teammate, thank you for the 40oz episode outside my parents' house before Junior prom, thank you for standing by me no matter the issue, thank you for playing that practical joke on me with the laxative gum, thank you for trying to teach me to dance, thank you for holding my legs while I reached for that A-Rod homerun in Camden Yards and almost crushed that little girl (*it's a baseball thing*). Thank you for picking me up from LaGuardia airport based only on a random voicemail. Thank you for the Houston experience. Thank you for all these great best friend memories. And thank you for being there when you didn't have to be. I love you brothers."

MORAL – Forget the whole enemies thing, just keep your friends as close as you can for as long as you can. You are going to need them.

℘

40 days, 40 years, 40 life lessons – Day 17

Dear Basil and Sabine,

I wish you could have known your great grandparents. James O. Melton and Ruth E. Jones of Newark, New Jersey and Albert "Ralph" Mann and Blanche Nabors of Croton-On-Hudson, New York. The Melton's of Newark raised 8 children, and were steadfast pillars in their community as well as in their church family at Mount Calvary Baptist Church where your great grandfather served as Deacon. Granddaddy or 'Diddy' as he was affectionately known by his children was born in Dothan, Alabama and worked in Newark, NJ as a postman. He drove a late model Mark Series Lincoln, black with red leather interior and it was like riding in a limousine whenever we were blessed to ride with Granddaddy. There is no argument that this man was the glue that held the Melton family to-gether. His quiet leadership and strength in God's love served as a rock solid foundation that will be forever unmoved. Sadly, I was not able to witness the beautiful splendor that was Ruth Edna Jones of Bennettsville, South Carolina as the lord called her home in 1973 to join his chorus of Angels soon after I was born. I am going to let Grandmama give you all those wonderful stories. Blanche Nabors of Ossining, New York loved bridge, gin-rummy, jazz and a good time. If there was a party, Grandma sure knew how to make it work. She was a classy woman, a caretaker and she didn't take any $h*t either. I saw her get upset once and there was No Way I was going to find out what twice looked like. And that leaves me with Ralph Mann – WHOAAA NELLY!

Albert "Ralph" Mann of Yonkers, New York was a carpenter by trade. He built his own home. He built 3 boats, SABEGE, SABEGE II, and Ms. Abigail. Legend has it after building boats named for 3 of his own children, **SA**ndy, **BE**rt and **GE**orge, he intended on building one for each of his grandchildren, the eldest being Abby Michael. I imagine if Grandpa were still with us he would be putting the finishing touches on Miss Morgana right now. He was a jazz musician who played tenor saxophone in the Bash Crawford Orchestra and once recorded with Cannoball Adderley. All those parties where Grandma was holding her glass and moving her hips, you would usually find Grandpa right there on his saxophone keeping the groove alive. My first few birthdays were held down by a jazz band right in the back yard. It was beautiful girls, just beautiful.

Many of my summers were spent out on Grandpa's boat SABEGE II, fishing in the Hudson River off of Croton Point. There was a little white house that sat above the hill where Grandpa would use as an anchor marker. We would sit out there for hours just passing the time with our lines in the water catching perch, bluefish, flounder and the occasional eel. On special days Grandpa would take us out crabbing. I call them special days because of the nature of the work, and make no mistake it was WORK. You have to set your traps and pull the rope up really, really fast when Grandpa would maneuver 'Miss Abigail' around to the trap marker. We would bring home the days catch and Grandma would be there in the kitchen with the hot water on boil. Mmmmmmmm, nothing quite like working for your dinner – makes it all taste so much better. Grandpa was also a connoisseur of smoked turkey. OMG! (*that is something young people say today*) he could smoke a turkey like nobody's business right in his own backyard on Riverview Trail.

Now, according to *your* Grandpa, my Dad, he would always regale different sayings that Grandpa would repeat, like, "A poor ride sure beats a proud walk," or my favorite, "Worry is interest paid on taxes that never come due." I try to keep that phrase at the forefront of my mind whenever I am faced with turmoil. I think you can actually use it when facing quite a few challenges in life. Of course it is going to mean different things to different people, but I think Grandpa was using that phrase to remind himself and others that there is no point to getting yourself all worked up over things when in the end the pieces are going to fall into place just as they are intended. And with Grandpa, that was just how life went. As I look back at my time with him and listen to my father talk about Grandpa I realize there sure was a whole heck of a lot of GOOD TIMES! And that was how life was for Grandpa and his family, one damn GOOD TIME. You'll probably find that some of these letters don't necessarily hold a life lesson per se, but I want you both to be mindful of a small story – one day a man was making inquiries about a young man named George who was applying for a job in the Katonah – Lewisboro school district. I've been told the conversation when something like this:

"Hey, do you know this kid?"

"Yeah, that's Ralph Mann's son, he comes from good stock."

"OK, he's hired."

MORAL – Know and appreciate your value. You are both Blue Chips.

40 days, 40 years, 40 life lessons –
Day 18

Dear Basil and Sabine,

Discipline is a part of life. There is self-discipline that you will have to use in order to keep yourself in line on a daily basis, but there is also the discipline handed out by parents that you will come to know as you grow older. Recently, while attending one of the 1,000 birthday parties you all seem to have every weekend I was talking with the father of one of your classmates; nice fellow, great dad. We were sitting there in the living room waxing poetic about how great you beautiful children are and how tasty the potato salad was when the father said something to me that gave me pause. He said, "man, these kids are so different today, if I ever talked to my mother the same way my own daughter talks to her mother, I would have been smacked in the face." Upon hearing these words dribble from his mouth my first reaction was to spread my fingers wide and do an impression of his mother, but then, I chilled (*Oran "Juice" Jones shout-out*). I digress. The bottom line here girls is that times have changed. And I am not sure for the better either.

The picture you have of Grandmama should never fade from being the beautiful, statuesque, kind, loving, strong, graceful image of womanhood that she is. Never! But, make no mistake she could handle "The Belt" like none other. Her dexterity and smooth, fluid motion from beginning to end of "whooping" was masterful. Look, I am exaggerating (*not really*) but you should understand that when I grew up, if you broke rules in the house or did something disrespectful – you were punished. There was no 'Time Out.' There would be no back and forth between parent and child. There was really only one option. The sequence went like this –

Step 1: Child does something wrong.

Step 2: Parent witnesses or hears about wrongdoing.

Step 3: Child braces for impact.

Step 4: Wailing begins.

Step 5: Siblings sit in other room laughing hysterically.

And with Grandmama, the most important step in the ENTIRE belt adjudication process was, and pay attention closely girls,

Step 6: Grandmama sits you down, looks right in your eyes, wipes away your tears and said the following, "You know this hurts me more than it does you right?!"

Step 7: You get a tight hug, walk out of the room and go face your laughing siblings with tears streaming down your face.

That was discipline. And don't think that Grandpa didn't get his either. That peaceful teddy bear of a man who gives you *zirberts* when you visit and gushes all over you any chance he gets could make your whole world come to a quick stop if you got him to the point of no return.

Today, discipline as doled out by the Grandmama's of the world has fallen by the wayside. Parents, as far as the ones I speak with do not utilize the belt, the switch, or the wooden spoon like days of old. We now try to match wits with our children or simply let them carry-on like this sort of behavior is O-K. It's not. We are doing you a disservice by not enforcing 'House Rules.' When I was a child there was an expectation of how I was supposed to behave both in and outside of the house and if I ran afoul of any of those rules, **action** was going to be taken. And make no mistake; action could have been taken by more individuals than just Grandmama. Remember what I said in letter #2, it takes a village. There was Mrs. Galloway, Aunt Verna, Aunt Pam; none of whom mind you are related by blood – each had authority to administer justifiable discipline. It is commonly referred to as In Loco Parentiis. And you know what, there was absolutely nothing wrong with any of that. Now girls, I am not saying that you are going to get spanked on a daily basis or you should live in fear of the belt. What I *am* saying is that when we talk about consequences and repercussions; just know that I am a firm believer in the philosophy of "this hurts me more than it hurts you."

MORAL – The belt had its place, just make sure **YOUR** actions keep it around my waist.

༆

40 days, 40 years, 40 life lessons – Day 19

Dear Basil and Sabine,

When I was 17 years old I worked for Bill Neave Landscaping. Mr. Neave was the father of one of my little league teammates, Scott Neave. Beautiful family, I still try to check in on Mr. Neave when I travel up to New York, he is a former Marine and he taught me a great deal about the value of hard work. One summer day I was working with two other men mowing lawns. It was toward the end of our work day and we got to one street that happened to be Mr. Neave's street, Sherwood Heights. There was one other house on the street that had to have the grass cut as well. The two men I was working with told me to start with the Neave lawn and they would go up the street to tackle the other home. They would meet me back at the Neave's when they were finished to help me wrap up. The homes weren't very far away from one another so I could see right where they were. So they dropped me off and I began to get to work. Now as was customary on these jobs you had to make sure you not only cut and edged the grass but also made sure the flowerbeds were free of weeds. It just so happens that at the Neave household there were just as many flowerbeds as there were blades of grass in the lawn it seemed. So I got to work on the first flowerbed down by the end of the driveway. I was good at pulling weeds; I worked fast and made sure not to disturb any of Mrs. Neave's plants.

I had only been working for a few minutes when I looked up and saw a New York State Trooper car pull into the driveway. The trooper got out of the car, walked toward me and asked me why I was hiding in the bushes? I dropped the weeds I was holding and said I wasn't hiding I was pulling weeds. He asked me to come toward the car with my hands where he could see them and I did. When I got to the car he told me to turn around and place my hands behind my back. I did. He then put his handcuffs on me and proceeded to ask me more questions about me hiding in the bushes. I told him I work for Bill Neave Landscaping just like the tan shirt with red letters indicated that I was wearing. I told him I was working with the crew that he could see up the street and that this was actually Bill Neave's house. He then asked me why I had broken into the house. I told him in fact that I had not. And at this point he opened up the back door of the police car and put me inside. As he walked around the house the co-workers who had been a few houses away were now barreling down the road to see what was going on. As they got out of the Bill Neave Landscaping truck they were driving, one of the men asked the trooper in quite a firm tone, "Why do you have our guy in your car?" The trooper responded, "I got a call of a house break-in and when I get here I see this black man hiding in the bushes." My head kind of slumped a bit in the backseat of the car when I heard this. At 17 I was very much aware of race; it had just rarely come up and 'punched' me in the face like that.

After a few more loooong minutes went by I heard a powerful truck engine coming up the street and then tires screeching as the truck came to a halt. Bill Neave made it from the door of his truck to the State Troopers nose in about 2 seconds. "You better get him out of that car right now before his mother gets here!" If I weren't so damn nervous I would have laughed. Bill has these steely blue-grey eyes and when he his angry these things can sort of pierce right through you; and at that moment he was giving the trooper the thousand yard stare. Bill explained that this was in fact his house and I was his employee. The trooper again explained the situation he came upon, but Bill would have nothing of it. What would come out later is that before we even arrived at the house, Bill's son Scott had come home from school without his house key and kicked in the side door to the house triggering the silent alarm and left before we got there. The trooper took me out of the car, unlocked the handcuffs and said, "I hope the rest of your day is uneventful." And then he left. End of story? …sort of, but not really.

The unfortunate thing here is that the story is still going. The story is benign in some chapters and horrific in others. The problem is that the story continues to grow. President Barack Obama was on television recently trying his best to explain elements of 'The Story', but there are going to be people who still don't understand its content. They are going to read the pages differently. As your parents, your mother and I have the responsibility to try and navigate you through your life as you get older such that you understand the context behind the story but ensure it doesn't detract from your overall growth and ability to take on and process much greater issues. It can't hinder you from anything you set your heart and mind to as it pertains to **your** success. We have to make sure the story becomes a history lesson and that you are able to write a completely different story, one free of racial bigotry and prejudice. This **has** to happen.

In that story I just told you, daddy was the only black person there that day, everyone else was white. Now go back and read it again and think about the actions of each individual very closely, actions free of color, yet full of morals and character if you can. I look at you girls in your classrooms as you play blissfully with all of your friends, friends who stem from a plethora of multicultural backgrounds and biracial families – nothing but laughter, friendship and shared learning free of ignorance and discrimination. And I like *that* story; there's more to gain from it.

MORAL – You *will* learn everything in Kindergarten and spend a lifetime trying to get back to when it was simple.

40 days, 40 years, 40 life lessons –
Day 20

Dear Basil and Sabine,

Somewhere around the age of six or seven years old I discovered the wonderful world of the movie theater. Along the stretch of Route 9 back in New York you had several different theaters to choose from. Beginning from Fishkill in the south you had the Dutchess Mall, they had 4 screens;

about 2 miles up the road was our drive-in theater (there's a strip mall there now); in Wappinger Falls we had the Imperial Plaza with 2 screens and the largest popcorn bin I have ever seen, they also had a coin dispenser on the side of the cash register where your change would roll down a little metal slide, and then further up the road was the South Hills Mall, they were the largest with I think 6 screens at the time. There was also the Juliet Theater in Poughkeepsie right next to Vassar College, but I only went there once or twice I believe – their floors were just too sticky.

Nevertheless, my movie theater christening consisted of films like Star Wars, Rocky, and the Bad News Bears. Going to the movie theater was an event for me. I paid attention to every detail from the ticket guy ripping your ticket in half to the way some popcorn was drenched with liquid butter. I loved every inch of the experience and when the movie was over I was usually reenacting movie scenes for the next 2 days. Even now I find myself quoting movie lines at least once a day: "It's easy to grin when your ship comes in, and you've got the stock market beat. But a man worthwhile is a man who can smile, when his shorts aren't too tight in the seat." (Classic!)

As promised, I said that on every 10th day I would provide you a list of some sort. Well today's list contains movies I think you should see when you are old enough to comprehend them. We are knocking out all of the appropriate G rated films now, Willy Wonka and the Chocolate Factory (*the Gene Wilder version*); the Lion King; Beauty and the Beast, the list goes on and on. But I fear that once you are old enough to watch PG-13 rated movies and eventually R-rated films you will miss out on a few cinematic classics that existed when I was growing up. These are movies that meant a lot to my life actually in some small way and have stayed with me. Now I know you are going to have **your** own experience and I don't mean to get in the way of that, but if you should have some free time and you want to see a few movies that Daddy likes, try these:

1. **Shawshank Redemption** (Perseverance and Friendship)
2. **Biloxi Blues** (I think I like it because the main character wants to be a writer)

3. **A Soldier's Story** (I wear a uniform to work every day and this speaks to me)
4. **Godfather** (It's just mandatory)
5. **Godfather II** (Same as 4)
6. **Four Weddings & a Funeral** (Pay particularly close attention to the funeral speech)
7. **St. Elmo's Fire** (Because every guy has a Dale Bieberman in his life)
8. **The Breakfast Club** (Wait until you are in high school to watch this)
9. **Sixteen Candles** (Trust me, you'll understand)
10. **Hav Plenty** (Another writer...oh yeah, LOVE 40 baby)
11. **Cooley High** (ummm, yup...one of the main characters likes to write)
12. **The Five Heartbeats** (Grandmama and Grandpa grew up with GREAT music)
13. **Field of Dreams** (Baseball is a metaphor for life...)
14. **She's Having a Baby** (The song at the end of the film kind of hits close to home)
15. **Love Actually** (Just pay attention to everything in this one...just in cases)
16. **Home for the Holidays** (Wow, family girls...FAMILY)
17. **Bingo Long Travelling All-Stars and Motor Kings** (Negro League Baseball, because Grandpa would want you to know this part of history)
18. **The Wiz** (I mean if you're going to watch a musical)
19. **Devil in a Blue Dress** (Because Don Cheadle is incredibly cool)
20. **Do the Right Thing** (Shelton Jackson Lee gets it right most of the time...)

These are just a few of my favorites, I have a ton more and if you look downstairs at all of my DVDs you will see what I am talking about. But again, if you have some time and want to see what Dad watched growing up, try some of these. You just might like a few.

MORAL – Movie night is my favorite night of the week with you two!

∽

40 days, 40 years, 40 life lessons –
Day 21

Dear Basil and Sabine,

Time. You will hear time described in many different phrases and ways. Time is money; time of day; time's a wasting; I wish I had more time, the list goes on and on for quite a long *time*! There will likely be moments in your life when you look back over the years and ask yourself where did all the time go? How did I all of the sudden wind up here? You sort of shake your head a bit and try to come up with a suitable answer to satisfy your bewilderment. Hopefully, you are able to pause and look back fondly over the past events of your life, knowing full well that you took most every opportunity to truly live 'In the Moment.' Conversely, in the case of a high school graduate like me, you could miss the essence of being in the moment and realize 20 years later at your high school reunion that you should have cherished those times just a bit more -- wishing you could go back in time and soak it all in for a few minutes longer.

On the day of my high school graduation I had to listen to several different speeches from a variety of people. There was the school Principal John Horgan, the Salutatorian (Barbara Wisniewski), the Valedictorian (Grace Shen) and the President of the School Board, you know him as Grandpa. Now I have a fairly good memory, and I remember that day in a series of snapshots, some are clear and some are not so clear. But there is one particular moment that plays like a loop in my head to this day and it wasn't until a few months ago that I began to fully grasp the meaning of it. As Grandpa was giving the lead in to his speech he addressed the students and said, "For some of you this is your formal graduation in life, remember that and be sure to act with dignity and class." Now I remember hearing it when he said it and I admit that I let it fly right by me, failing in that moment to understand the extent to what that particular sentence could really mean throughout my own life.

When the day comes that you are standing at the formal ceremony celebrating **your** departure from high school, try to grasp if you can the fact that you are now taking leave from your childhood, saying farewell to childhood friends, and you are now moving to your next level and taking with you an armament of achievement that you have now placed in your tool belt. This tool belt is going to be with you for the rest of your life. It is up to you to ensure your tool belt is filled with all of the necessary items to keep building **you**. Try as best you can to soak in this moment and understand the importance of **your** achievement. It's yours, you earned it. There are plenty of people, both family and friends who have supported you along the way and we are looking forward to seeing you achieve more. This is your time.

When I look back at myself on my high school graduation day, I remember being happy -very happy. And I want you both to have that same feeling surrounded by all of your friends and family celebrating with you. I hope that on that day I am able to look you in the eyes, give you a tight hug and be in *that* moment with you. I don't want to look at you and think to myself, 'where did all the time go? where did my little girls go?' Just let me hug you a little tighter before sending me home and you head out with your friends to celebrate. But remember it. Cherish it. Put it all in a jar and place it on the shelf, because there will come a day when you wish you could just close your eyes and go back for just one moment of time.

MORAL – Try to listen more when Grandmama and Grandpa are speaking, they have the benefit of time and wisdom.

ᕣ

40 days, 40 years, 40 life lessons – Day 22

Dear Basil and Sabine,

I am going to spend the next several letters writing to you about college. And the reason I have to do this over a series of letters is based on the fact that I have a truckload of things to offer you about the college experience, well, *my* college experience anyway. Now let me say right up front that I am no expert on college, quite far from it actually. But, I do know how to get into college and I also know how to get out of college, albeit eventually. What I need to talk to you both about is what goes on in between your first day and your last day. However, before I get too far down the road here, let me sort of shape the scene for you.

Right around the early spring of your senior year in high school you will start to receive notices from the colleges you have applied to. This will be a very exciting, yet anxious time for you. You are likely to have a favorite university or two that you would like to attend and there may also be what you call, 'safe' schools mixed in there, the ones you feel you will get into without any trouble. And should things go well, you will stroll out to that mailbox one afternoon, open the little door and see a nice thick envelope staring you in the face. You see a thin envelope usually doesn't say what you want it to. Now Daddy applied to about 6 colleges and the one that was a bit of a stretch was a school nestled east of the Shenandoah Valley amongst the foothills of Albermarle County called The University of Virginia. Now I had heard of this school once or twice before while in high school. I recall 2 people, David Edwards and Lee Ann Campbell from John Jay getting accepted there. It was impressed upon me that getting into UVa was akin to writing your own ticket. Meaning once you are in – you are on a glide path to success.

Now one day before I began writing my college applications, Grandpa and I hopped into the Chrysler Minivan and headed south. We hit Towson State (*not for me*), drove past Howard University (*a bit too busy for this upstate NY kid*), had an appt. at Hampton University (*I don't think jeans and a t-shirt work here*); then over the bridge to Old Dominion (*Dad, can we go back to Hampton right quick*), and then we ventured out to a school in Blacksburg, VA called Virginia Tech, (*hey Dad, do you smell that?*) and well, we just kept it moving. The very last school we would visit on this trip was UVa on a very early Sunday morning in the Fall of 1990. It was quiet, minimal souls were about the dew covered grounds, the leaves on the lawn were turning colors and it reminded me of home. The place looked perfect and so did our tour guide (*Thank you Lee Ann*). SOLD! I wanted to go to the University of Virginia. I couldn't get home fast enough to begin writing the application. I toiled over that thing for days, trying to get it just right -- 1st draft, 2nd draft, 3rd draft. Grandmama and Grandpa would read, proofread, reread and I just kept trying to get it right. And then, it was ready. Stuff it in an envelope, lick a few stamps, and place in the mail… and wait…and wait… and wait.

Right around late March I received a letter in the mail inviting prospective students to something called Spring Fling at UVa. I was immediately perplexed. Prospective? Wait a second, I took Latin, I think prospective means I am intended to be there. Did they really just send this letter before the acceptance letter? What a way to play with my emotions. Don't they realize between girls, acne, and Public Enemy I don't need this kind of emotional angst? Well, about 2 days later I went out to the mailbox at the end of the driveway, opened that little door and there it was… The Fattest Envelope Ever! Dear Bashon W. Mann, you're the coolest, you're the best, you had us at hello, come and dance around the Rotunda with us! Are you kidding me? *Cue the music again…. DANCIN, DANCIN, DANCIN MACHINE, WATCH ME GET DOWN, WATCH ME GET DOWN… AS IT DO, DO, DO, DO, DO ON THE SCENEEEEEEE… I got into college!

Girls, I went down to this thing called Spring Fling and after 3 days I knew one thing for sure, college was going to be fun, fun and more fun. You know the first person I ever met at UVa? This guy named Rahman Branch, yup, Uncle Rock. Grandpa and daddy were looking for a dorm called Balz and we saw this **big** guy in a Redskins starter jacket throwing a football. I said Dad let's ask him. Excuse me, can you tell me where Balz Dormitory is? This guy turned around with the biggest smile I had ever seen and he said, oh yeah, come with me. I've been on 'Team Rock' ever since. (*more on Rock later*)

OK, I should probably wrap this first letter up. So, I came home from UVa excited and euphoric beyond words. I couldn't wait to get back down there. UVa was all I could think about, so much so that I forgot about my 4th quarter of high school. Would you believe that somehow UVa got a hold of my grades from my last quarter at John Jay? Yup, they sure did. And lo' and behold, I went out to the mailbox one day after high school graduation and would you believe a really skinny envelope was in there waiting for me from the University of Virginia:

Dear Bashon W. Mann, YOU ARE NOT AS COOL AS YOU THINK YOU ARE, PLEASE CHECK YOURSELF AND YOUR GRADES AND SHOW US YOU REALLY MEAN BUSINESS, BECAUSE AS OF RIGHT NOW YOU ARE ON ACADEMIC NOTICE BASED ON YOUR LAST QUARTER PERFORMANCE IN HIGH SCHOOL. PLEASE PROVIDE A WRITTEN EXPLANATION OF YOUR POOR GRADES.

MORAL – When you lose focus, the wrong things become clear.

⤸

40 days, 40 years, 40 life lessons – Day 23

Dear Basil and Sabine,

When I was about 11 years old a television show appeared on NBC that became quite popular. It was called, The Cosby Show. It came on Thursday nights at 8pm. Suffice it to say, each and every Thursday night for 8 years my world stopped when the Cosby Show came on. In addition to George Mann, Linda Mann, Dwayne Mann, and Carolyn Jacobs, I had a whole other family to deal with in my life; my Thursday night parents were Cliff and Claire and my brothers and sisters were named Saundra, Denise, Theo, Vanessa, and Rudy. I also had two close friends named Cockroach and Kenny aka Bud. Now as this show grew year after year, I grew along with it. And one day my pseudo older sister Denise went to pseudo college (Hillman). And someone at NBC decided that at 8:30pm they would devote time to show how Denise was coping with her college experience, her 'Different World.' Now I watched this show closely, but I apparently didn't listen to Aretha Franklin close enough when she sang the opening credits to the show: (*YouTube the Different World Theme song when you have a moment.*)

In the Fall of 1991 I stepped onto the grounds of the University of Virginia, ready to begin my college years. I practically pushed Grandmama and Grandpa out of my dorm room and back into their car (*dumb move, remember what I said about time*). I was just ready to sink my teeth into all that fun I remember from that Spring Fling extravaganza. I knew it was going on somewhere and I had to go find it. But apparently UVa had other things on tap before any of the parties started; there was this whole 'go to class' thing. You actually had to register for classes and buy books to read and things like that. There were dorm meetings and mentor meetings and food plans to purchase. There were all these other things I had to do that felt a whole lot like work. "Hey! I want the Fling man! Where's the Fling Thing?!" Well, I settled in and followed the crowd to Old Cabell Hall. I bought books, I bought a meal plan, and I went to class. Wait a minute; I got that last sentence wrong. Grandmama and Grandpa bought books, Grandmama and Grandpa bought a meal plan, they were five states away and I began to go to classes that they paid for through something called tuition. I believe for out of state students tuition was $11,286 per year in 1991.

Now for the most part, in the beginning things went smoothly. I lived in an area called Old Dorms, Emmett 210 was my dorm room and I shared it with a young man from Mars. Yup, Darryl Cobb was from Mars, Pennsylvania and he wanted to be an Engineer. Remember what I said to you about Kareem Montague? About paying attention to the smart people in the room – well the same thing applies to Darryl and we shared the same room for two years. If Daddy was a bit more astute back then I would have paid more attention to how Darryl approached Engineering, particularly his study habits. In Emmet 209 Daddy met two young men from Cleveland, Ohio, Kenny Surratt and David Stewart. I had never met anyone from Ohio before and these two did not disappoint. As some people might say, they 'repped' for their city! (*Shout out to TDK productions!*). The four of us held it down for Emmet quite properly. We have a lot of shared memories together, **a lot**. (**Sidenote:** If someone ever tells you that you can make all the long distance calls you want for free just by using a two digit code, do *not* believe it!)

Now my first year of college consisted of many different self-discoveries. I met new people, began new friendships, saw new things, did new things, some of them not so good in fact; I partied, I drank, I smoked and started doing things that I would never have done back in Wappinger Falls, back where my parents were, 5 states away. I was on my own and I was adjusting to my Different World. I struggled to wake up and go to class from time to time (*Grandmama wasn't there to wake me anymore*), however I understood that the main objective here was to actually get grades, passing grades and my eyes, when open, for the most part were still on the prize.

I was able to get through my first year of college without much harm or unfortunate circumstance, but I was beginning to change. I was a little older, not necessarily wiser and I had now experienced what it feels like to be a big fish coming from a little pond and falling into a much larger body of water with fish that were just as big if not *bigger* than I was. And if you don't wrap your head around the fact that whoever you were in high school has *no bearing* whatsoever on your status in college then let me be the first to tell you. It means nada. There are thousands of other Class Presidents, thousands of other Homecoming Court participants, thousands of other most popular kids in class. You are not special, not to anyone there anyway. And you know what, no matter how hard you try to show how special (read: *crazy*) you can be, you really just start to become a distorted image of the person you truly are, the person you were before the car turned onto 29 South. So should you ever feel yourself faced with the dilemma of operating outside of your comfort zone or compelled to begin taking risks you wouldn't normally have taken under George and Linda's roof or Cliff and Claire's for that matter, try to remember the expectations of the one's writing the check. In this particular transaction a bill of sale will be requested and typically the buyer wants it framed. Try not to forget this, because they won't.

I will stop there for today. I think you are starting to get the picture.

MORAL – It's a *Different World* but remember you'll have the tool belt to handle it. Just trust **YOUR** tools.

℘

40 days, 40 years, 40 life lessons – Day 24

Dear Basil and Sabine,

One of the greatest upsides to your college experience will be the new people you meet and the friendships you forge. I was fortunate to meet an assortment of good peoples, some of whom I am close with today. They were from all over the place too. Chicago; Atlanta; Philadelphia; Cleveland; South Orange, New Jersey; the Bronx; Brooklyn; Richmond; Washington D.C.; NoVa, and all places in between. And, because you are meeting these people at a time when your eyes are opening to a new time in your life you will establish certain bonds with folks who become quite close as they are going thru similar and sometimes shared experiences. These friendships, if you are lucky, can often last a lifetime. Now understand some of them won't for one reason or another. But I think as you get older and life becomes a bit clearer you will realize that silly things done between 18 and 21 don't really mean much north of 40. And, if you find that someone still holds a grudge for things you did back in college, well, that's just something you will have to let go of. Life has a way of showing you there is a bit more to it than those trivial moments.

But the friends that do **stick** – the ones that see in you a bit more than what is on the surface, well they will stand with you through your growing pains, through your selfish antics and all the other sometimes dumb and moronic things you do even past the age of 21, only to see you come out clean on the other side and that's a wonderful thing. You will hear me describe a few of these people as the 'fellas' or more importantly your Uncles by proxy. There's Uncle Rock, Uncle Gabe, Uncle Carl, Uncle Wes,

Uncle Dele, Uncle Doug, Uncle Damion, Uncle Cov, Uncle Will, Uncle Dude, Uncle Mike, Uncle Randy, Uncle Raz, Uncle Dana, Uncle Holbrook, Uncle Sweat, Uncle Slim, Uncle Tone, Uncle Boo, Uncle Kev, Uncle Twaun, and several more, the crew rolled deep. You see these individuals knew me at a very young age and we all matured (*eventually*) and grew around one another through some shifting times in our lives. There was laughter, there was pain, there was anger, there was fighting and then there was more laughter, often raucous laughter. We went from 17 to 40+ and we are now a mix of fathers, husbands, teachers, lawyers, doctors, musicians, military officers, businessmen, and business owners who still call on one another to check in and see how the other is doing, making sure things are all right. Because each of us knows that sometimes throughout life there are going to be curveballs that brush you back a bit and sometimes you just need a little help getting back in the batter's box, ready for the next pitch.

As my college years drew on, these 'fellas' shared in creating a lot of really good memories. Road trips to Myrtle Beach, Howard Homecoming, Virginia Beach, Freaknic; trips back to New York over se-mester break – they were shared life experiences that I will always hold on to. But let me be clear here girls – remember what I said about class being a priority? Well you see road trips to all of these nice locations away from the grounds of UVa will ultimately keep you from focusing on and even attending those classes, and if you find that the people on these road trips change but you are the only constant, well then there stands to reason you are the one who is in fact 'tripping' and in need of a reality check. Realize that the onus is not upon your friends to steer you in the direction you should have been heading all along. When you don't go to class, nothing happens to them. When you don't get good grades, nothing happens to them. When you don't accept *your* respon-sibilities, nothing will happen to them and nothing *good* will happen for **you**. From the moment you enter college, you will have choices to make. Do I go to class or do I stay in bed; Do I go on that road trip or do I finish that paper – too many of the **wrong** choices and you will find that you have a dug a hole so deep semester after semester, year after year, that you won't be able to find a ladder tall enough to get yourself out. And your friends who made the time to study, who said 'no' to the last road trip will simply have to move on without you. They have their own lives to live and they are not required to keep a safety rope handy to pull you out of a hole you dug.

Yes, college is a fun time and yes you will have a road trip or two with dear friends; I am not saying not to. However, I need you to have a full understanding that your college experience is one that can either be the best time in your life or border on perhaps the worst. That is a choice you have to make for yourself.

MORAL – Believe me when I say the parties and road trips are more enjoyable when the papers are done and the grades are in.

♋

40 days, 40 years, 40 life lessons – Day 25

Dear Basil and Sabine,

HAHAHAHAHAHAHAHAHAHAHAHAHAHAHAHAHAHAHAHAHA! You know what that sound is? It's the sound of laughter on the day of your college graduation. It's the sound of pure joy at the elation of finally completing such a huge milestone. It's the sound of proud parents and relatives celebrating and showing their continued support for you. It's the sound all of my friends were making; only I wasn't with them to hear it. I was back at home in New York serving a one year academic suspension from UVa. Ouch! The DJ was no longer playing that music and my dancing came to a halt. All of the excitement I had trying to get into college was now a distant memory, as I had to imagine what could and what should have been. *"OK wait; stop Dad, why are you telling us this? Why can't these college letters be more inspiring and light-hearted?"* Well I cannot drive this story home enough, so listen closely to what I have to say. I will use every fiber of my being to ensure you both understand and learn from every pitfall and wrong turn I made. You may choose to ignore them, but you will know what it takes to avoid or push through the challenges and obstacles in front of you; whether by your own doing or otherwise. I owe you this.

Daddy came back home for that year and made an attempt to get back to square one so I might return to UVa and ultimately finish what I had started. I took a job as a treasury analyst with American Intl. Group in Manhattan, and for a minute I had forgotten about stepping away from college. I was making 41k in salary and decided I would buy a car to get around. You know that silver Mercedes Benz that sits down in the garage? Well uh, yeah I bought that as a little *'hey look at me, I may not have a degree but you don't have one of these'* prize. Acts of insecurity and self-consciousness will slowly pull you down to your knees, drowning in your own tears if you aren't careful – MESSAGE! But I played out my new day-to-day routine, commuting into Grand Central Station, hopping on the A, C train down to Wall Street, becoming part of the working class. I enjoyed it. Suit and tie, briefcase, power lunches, and happy hours at the Shark Bar, I wore it well. But then there were the trips back down to UVa to see old friends and I realized just how bad I missed being there *and* how much they didn't care about the car I drove to get there. As much as I tried to act like I was cool, like I had simply taken a little "break" from the school scene, I was clearly in disarray.

When it finally came time for me to head back to UVa I convinced Grandmama and Grandpa that I had it all together and the year off from school had taught me a valuable lesson. Daddy was a good liar. I had even convinced myself that was true. I arrived back on those grounds with the intention of trying to get it right, but I was too far gone by that point. I gave it that ole college 2nd try for about a month and then simply threw in the towel and let it all just fall apart. By the time finals came around I made a feeble attempt to convince the Dean to let me take a comprehensive exam to account for all of my missed midterms, papers, and class work. Not just for 1 class but for 5. She almost threw me out of her office. If I could find her today I would take her to dinner and offer her a sincere thank you for finally drawing a line in the sand and making it very clear that I had a decision to make – a decision that had nothing to do with the University of Virginia. I had to make a life decision.

When it dawned on me that I would have to call Grandmama and Grandpa to tell them what I had done I felt the weight of the world on my shoulders. How could I have let it come to this? Their disappointment was going to be more than I was willing to face. Solution – Don't call, just disappear. When their phone calls and messages went unreturned I knew I was facing a dead end. I was scared to face my own parents. In desperation I pulled out a phone book and searched for travel agent numbers, as I considered leaving the country. I was that far gone. In a moment of clarity I moved from Travel Agent to Armed Forces and found the address for the local recruiting station on Route 29. I came in on 29, looks like I would be going out on it too! I ran from my Shamrock Apt bldg. all the way to the parking lot of the recruitment center just behind a Super Fresh grocery store and a Taco Bell. When I stood in the parking lot facing those recruiter doors from about 50 yards away I had another choice to make – Army (*mmm, no.*); Air Force (*no interest in flying*); Marines (*I play a good crazy, but…*); Navy (*hmmm, Bill Cosby, John Coltrane, George Jefferson…yes, Weezy's husband all served in the Navy*) – yada, yada, yada I work for the Chief of Naval Operations now.

I can certainly share with you the details of what happened when I entered that recruiter's office that day. Be sure to ask me some time and I won't spare a word. There's a woman named TM2 Kathleen Walsh who should get an award for most compassionate recruiter of the year for how she handled me coming into her office dripping with sweat and demanding enlistment papers and a plane ticket. I won't forget her. As for Grandmama and Grandpa, well that's another interesting story. You should ask Uncle Gabe and Uncle Kev how that one played out in front of them. For now I want you both to take away one important thing: that no matter how difficult the circumstance may be, Mommy and Daddy *need* you to know that you can **always** come to us. We will work through the problem together.

MORAL – A mother's love knows no distance, especially from Wappinger Falls to Shamrock Road, Apt 15.

⚘

40 days, 40 years, 40 life lessons – Day 26

Dear Basil and Sabine,

And so on June 3, 1996 a college dropout from Wappinger Falls, NY arrived in Great Lakes, Illinois and became Seaman Recruit Mann, Division 290; Ship 2. For the next nine weeks I was in Navy boot camp, destined for a date with submarine training upon completion. But what I have learned time and time again girls is that there are typically larger things at play throughout your life and no matter how hard you try to go one way, life has a way of pulling you in the direction you might never thought you were intended to go when you took the first step of your journey. And when you allow yourself to think with an open mind you will be surprised what opportunities come your way.

Here I had fought so hard to get out of town as soon as I could to avoid facing my parents; I accepted the first job that I qualified for as a sonar technician on a submarine. But then life came along and turned me a different way. Would you believe just 2 weeks before I finished boot camp, the Navy Ceremonial Honor Guard asked me to come to Washington DC and become a body bearer? I was ecstatic and honored to do so. Washington DC?!?! Where are all my friends from UVa had gone after graduation? This is great, what could possibly go wrong right? Well, it wasn't so much that anything went wrong, it's just that things were not yet quite as right as they should have been. You see, when you get to a point in your life when you haven't accepted responsibility for where *you* are and you try to make excuses and 'fake it, till you make it', often times you will find that all that faking goes on so long and you fail to realize you will NEVER make it to anything. You can't lie to yourself, your friends and your family portraying a false reality before one day finding that it's hard to wake up and face your own image in the mirror looking back at you. And then1996 becomes 1999 and you really haven't moved yourself forward, all you have done really is mark time while simply standing still. Eventually, if you are fortunate enough, without any notice at all the larger thing in life happens for you. For me it came in the form of BRAC, Base Realignment and Closure, to a little place on the map called Millington, TN.

And so there I was, rolling west on Interstate 40 to my new duty location. Daddy cruised over the Virginia line, through the mountains of Knoxville, TN, passed the Ole Opry of Nashville, driving my white, '89 Cadillac Coupe Deville (*where's the Benz playa?!*) past a cotton field and onto Naval Support Activity Mid-South in the middle of a tornado warning. It was June 1999 and this was to be home for a while. I found out within just a couple of months that there are really just a few things to do while stationed in Millington. You can go to work, come home, and sleep; you can go to work, come home and drink, then sleep; *or* you can go to work and then go Back To School! So after drinking too much and sleeping even more, daddy walked into the Navy Tuition Assistance office three years after walking into a Navy recruiter's office and said, "Ma'am, I'd like to get my college degree." And in August of 1999 I became a junior at the University of Memphis. This would become my new routine – go to work, go to school, come home, **study** and then sleep. I was finally on my own and doing what I needed to do for myself. And, I was paying the bill, 25% of it anyway. So I was going to get my money's worth and then some.

I wrote this particular series of letters to you girls so that you would see a part of my life that I don't talk about much with anyone else and that I am not particularly proud of. I had family and very close friends to whom I lied to throughout many of those years just to cover up my own failings and irresponsibility when I didn't have to. They would have loved me just the same if I were upfront with them. Throughout the course of your life there are going to be plenty of mistakes that you will make along the way, but that is ok – it's human and you will recover from them. What you want to make sure of is that you *learn* from those mistakes so that once they are made you can put them in your past and move forward without looking back at them, without letting them haunt you or hinder you from your intended growth. One day you may choose that you wish to go to college and on that day when you arrive on campus or on Grounds (*hint, hint*), right before you push me away to leave and get back in the car I am going give you one last hug and hand you these last four letters and I want you to keep them close. Let them serve as your alarm clock to keep you getting up for class.

MORAL – Sometimes walking away from what is SAFE and FAMILIAR is really you walking toward what is meant to be.

40 days, 40 years, 40 life lessons –
Day 27

Dear Basil and Sabine,

On July 28, 1968 in Newark, New Jersey a slender young woman dressed in a modest, yet elegant white dress, stood stoically alongside a svelte young man from Croton-On-Hudson, New York wearing a white tuxedo jacket with black pants and before God, the Reverend J. Wendell Mapson, Sr., of Mount Calvary Baptist Church, family and friends, they were wed -- making this day, July 28th 2013 their 45th wedding anniversary.

George Wyatt Mann and Linda Melton Mann are your incredibly lovely grandparents, my mom and dad, and though I have mentioned them time and time again throughout these letters and you know them and love them dearly, let me take a moment to tell you a little bit about what their love for each other means to me. And please, let me again add the caveat here that I am 1. No expert on love and 2. No expert on marriage – but I am a bit of a savant on the boundless appreciation of two people loving one another and their family, providing undying love and support such that their children, nieces, nephews and friends can relish in the blessings these two have received as a couple. It is an unselfish display of love, admiration, tolerance, forgiving, and caring for each other that is oh so rare in the world today.

Grandmama and Grandpa once told me that in all their years of marriage if you added up all of the bad days you would probably find there were 2 full years of heartache and strain within their marriage, still leaving an abundance of overwhelmingly pleasant, happy and fulfilling *good* times, I know, I saw plenty of them. I have never let that little nugget of wisdom go. The one thing I truly appreciate about my parents is that despite any low points they may have faced between the two of them they made sure their children came first. Our needs were always met and we became the center point to which their focus of love was aimed. Those matters which needed to be handled in private between husband and wife were just that – private and between the two of them.

There are not enough words in Webster's dictionary for me to describe how I feel about my parents. They have sacrificed so much for me and my siblings from the beginning and are still there to offer all of themselves for our benefit and the benefit of their grandchildren despite asking for anything in return but respect. As my father said to me recently, you'll find that as your girls get older, all the worry, the concern... it never ends, it just never ends. Today I think back to all of the times I know for a fact I gave them worry and wonder how in those moments; coupled with the thousands of other times I have absolutely no clue about, were they ever able to make it through without going completely insane. And I guess the answer, or at least the answer I want to believe is that they had each other to lean on for strength. They are the best one-two punch in the business and they can put together quite the combination when they need to. Most importantly however was the fight they waged to keep their hearts locked no matter the hardship. Your grandparents have made me a believer of love -- that love conquers all things, and while fairytale endings with Prince charming and even Colin Firth for that matter may be just the thing of movies, I do believe that ever after is indeed a reality worth considering, just in cases.

One day several years ago daddy was talking with Grandpa about his new boat and he said that one of the better features was the double seat Captain's chair. Grandpa said, "it means a lot to have your First Mate sitting right there next to you, you'll understand it as you get a little older."

MORAL – Happy 45th Anniversary Mom and Dad, may you be in love, wonderfully ever after!

40 days, 40 years, 40 life lessons -
Day 28

Dear Basil and Sabine,

When I was quite younger I knew in my head that I would be a professional basketball player. Most every day I would find myself out in the driveway about to take the last shot in the 4th quarter of a tie game to win the championship. Each game ended with me hitting the winning shot;

even when I missed, the 'do over' rule allowed me to reclaim champion-ship glory. Grandpa went along with my NBA dreams and would be out there showing me the finer points of the layup, the jump-shot, and how to use my left hand. Whenever I would sit down for breakfast and Grandpa would be there eating his toast and coffee I'd ask him if I could drink some of his coffee. He would reply the same way each time, "coffee will stunt your growth." And I wanted to be 7'0" tall, so I stayed as far away from coffee as I could. Oddly enough, I believed Grandpa so much that I still don't drink coffee today (*I love Haagen-Dazs Java Chip though*). But hey, when you want something, you want it right? And I wanted to be tall.

Now Uncle Dwayne and Cousin Carolyn had different dreams and I could never quite understand their persistence with their career interests so early in life. I mean basketball seemed like fun, the NFL seemed like fun, and Major League Baseball seemed like fun. Why would anyone want to do anything else in life but play professional sports and make a bazil-lion dollars and buy anything they want, right?!? So when Uncle Dwayne said pretty much at birth that he wanted to be in theatre and act in plays I laughed at him and when Cousin Carolyn said she wanted to be a pe-diatrician by the 4th grade I blew her off and paid no attention to it. It all seemed quite foolish and beyond my realm of comprehension. I had a championship to win out in the driveway and the clock was ticking.

Well girls, you know what's funny? Playing in the MLB, NFL, or NBA takes a whole heck of a lot of natural God-given talent, and *practice*. Yup, I'm talkin' 'bout PRACTICE! And I don't mean hitting the winning shot in the driveway, I mean getting up day after day after day and doing the same drills over and over and over again. The drills that are not fun, the drills that have nothing to do with winning the game at the buzzer, but everything to do with being able to play the game right from beginning to end. And apparently this theory doesn't just apply to sports. You have to practice in most any career you choose if you want to be successful – You have to develop your passion. Uncle Dwayne went to theater camp every summer and joined theatre clubs so that he could become better at his passion. Cousin Carolyn took a job as a candy striper in St. Francis

Hospital so that she could be closer to her passion. When the drills became more work than fun I stopped going after my pursuit of playing in the NBA. To make matters worse, I hadn't reached 7'0" tall by the time I was 14 so I felt basketball may not be my future. I became less passionate.

And so I easily let that dream go. I didn't believe in it. I didn't want it enough. When your mother and I tell you that you can be most anything you choose to be in life, I want you to believe it with all of your heart. At 6 and 4 that may sound bizarre, but I want you to know it **now**; I want you to believe it now. Because I want it to sink in and let it become a part of your make up. You know I laughed at Uncle Dwayne and Cousin Carolyn all those years ago but I have the utmost respect for each of them today, you know why? Right now, Uncle Dwayne is studying for his Doctorate in Theatre at Northwestern University and Cousin Carolyn; well she is Dr. Carolyn Jacobs, MD; Pediatrician at University of Rochester Children's Hospital.

MORAL – Listen to Lena Horne in the Wiz as she sings, 'Believe in Yourself.' It's great theme music.

⚘

40 days, 40 years, 40 life lessons - Day 29

Dear Basil and Sabine,

In one of your earlier letters I made reference to the teachers you would encounter throughout your life. I talked about the people you would come across in the larger classroom of life, those who would provide you with additional learning experiences to carry you forward. Well in the 16 years I have spent in the Navy I have come in contact with several people who served in that capacity quite abundantly. These individuals took the time to put me under their wing and with incredible patience showed me the pathway to career progression and life skills even when I was adamant about looking in the other direction. Each and every one of them were true leaders and have worn their uniform and performed their duties with honor and substance of character. I am proud to have served with them.

The first officer I ever met within my profession was CDR Anthony Cooper, a man of large stature with an even larger smile who ensured me that my success in the Navy was based solely upon my desire to generate the energy to create it; his guidance and tutelage continues to be sought after today. LT Brad Fagan set the example for me as a "mustang" Division Officer while I was still enlisted; he gave me the confidence to consider becoming a naval officer by simply telling me the truth. There was CDR Dave Werner who instilled the philosophy of being an asset to your account holders and owning your Public Affairs issues, he is a great man who adores his family; everyone knows Chad and Hannah have a great father. CDR Steve Lowry was a gentle giant who with his introspective wisdom and full-bellied laugh could disarm most any a hostile situation within seconds; I learned to be human from him. And then there is Captain Cate Mueller who I watched quite closely without her knowing, who showed me that family and Navy are two great tastes that go good together. I wish I could list all of my great shipmates here, but I am afraid there may not be enough space on the Internet for their names and all of the great things I have to say about them. The ones I cherish know full well who they are and what they mean to me and what they have meant to my Navy career. But with this letter I would like to talk to you both about 2 individuals that had a profound effect on me while in uniform.

When Daddy went to Officer Candidate School in Pensacola, FL I had the great fortune to cross paths with a man who on his best day in impressively shined boots and a Smokey bear cover reached the middle of my chest. He was Marine Corps First Sergeant Terry Jones, my OCS drill instructor, who brought more out of me physically and mentally than I ever thought I had within me. On the eve preceding a make-up failed Room, Locker, and Personnel Inspection I became so flustered by the notion of failing I called Grandmama sobbing almost uncontrollably on the pay phone (*these are phones you used to put coins in to talk*). Looking back I realize exactly why I was so emotional. I had an appropriately placed fear of First Sergeant Jones and was afraid of letting him down. And it had nothing to do necessarily with physical intimidation mind you; I just didn't ever want to disappoint the man. You see, Marines have a way about them. They carry with them a respect for what they do and who they are that tends to raise just a thin layer above the other services. And I say this with utmost respect of all my service brethren. I see it daily in how they wear their uniform. Their walk is different. And Sergeant Jones made sure Honor Class 18-02 walked tall with our heads high and our chests out.

Sergeant Jones and I once shared a unique interaction when I placed a special liberty request to visit your mother one weekend. He called me over the mess deck PA system and demanded I meet him in the corridor. My 6'1" frame approached this 5'7" Marine hesitantly and leaned in for his message. While I can't share the language with you now, you should know that despite how I felt about seeing your Mom, I couldn't shake Sergeant's Jones words and face from my head the entire weekend, specifically his last sentence. "You better remember this weekend, cause Monday morning you will be paying for it." But I lived to tell you about it, so there's that little victory. Sergeant Jones was a motivator, he took young college graduates and he made sure they understood what the Navy needed and expected from its young officers and he made it his duty to deliver the best Navy Ensigns he possibly could. One of my favorite movies not to make it on your list is an Officer and A Gentleman. Well, First Sergeant Jones, USMC my OCS drill instructor made me into an officer and I was honored to receive his first salute for what he did for me. Every cadence I sing as I run is a tribute to him.

The second individual is Captain Rick Smethers. When Capt Smethers and I met I don't think he liked me very much. As a matter of fact I think he almost said as much. And I kind of knew where he was coming from. I arrived at his command as a boot Ensign fulfilling my first assignment as an officer. Now I didn't know much about Navy SEALs, but Capt Smethers didn't know much about me either. What I will always remember is our first interaction outside my office one day on the Phil Bucklew Center grinder soon after I checked onboard. Capt Smethers stood in my doorway blocking the sunlight and laid out his feelings for me, explaining that his thoughts were not personal.

I was replacing a PAO he had grown comfortable with and now he was compelled to espouse his displeasure with how the powers that be might have made a mistake on this one. The one-sided conversation went down another road that without going into too much detail captured the Captain's thoughts about being in the position he was after a career as an operator with a distinct group of individuals. Let's just say with a war going on, there were other places the Captain felt he could be useful. As Capt Smethers spoke at length about his career and the places he had been, I realized I was standing alongside quite an extraordinary individual, someone who would face insurmountable danger with the knowledge and belief that freedom and democracy are worth laying down your life for. I have no doubt his peers and friends would agree he was a special man; there are not many who fit his mold.

Once he finished relaying what he needed to say I then reached down for whatever courage I had left in my soul and told Capt Smethers what he needed to hear based on the knowledge I had gained from previous PAOs under which I had been in command. "Captain, it's your job to reach these young men at BUD/S and provide these future operators a true example of what it means to be a SEAL; that is why you are here." I can still hear those words escaping my lips and floating out into the sea salt air. Captain Smethers looked down at me with these penetrating, beady eyes of his and pretty much without saying a single word relayed to me, "Who the F@#& are you?" At that moment I did my best new guy impression staring right back, also not saying a word but somehow answering, "I'm your new Ensign." He shook his head a little before walking off and well -- we got along great as far as I am concerned. There are a great deal of other stories I would love to relay to you about my times talking with and listening to Capt Smethers but if I tell you, well -- then I'd have to hug you. The bottom line is that Capt Smethers is a man I greatly respect and I wish the country could know what he and his family sacrificed in support of our security as a Nation. Many will never know and even more will take it for granted.

Girls, men and women fight and die for this country because they believe in a greater principle of democracy upon which we were founded. It does not mean our country is perfect, it means we must each push forward together to ensure our freedoms for the pursuit of a more perfect union are protected. You are encouraged to travel this world of ours, travel as often as you can, but should you choose to call this place home, know there are individuals willing to give the ultimate sacrifice so that we ALL can live, speak, pray, and love freely and respectfully.

MORAL – There are those who have gone before you whose shoulders you both stand upon. Honor their sacrifice in all your success.

ೞ

40 days, 40 years, 40 life lessons – Day 30

Dear Basil and Sabine,

I grew up in a musical household. There was music everywhere; in the car, at the backyard parties and pumping on both floors during Saturday morning chores. Grandpa was a WBLS 107.5 man, but I was partial to 98.7 KISS FM. I still have a registered KISS card in my possession. I spent many a Friday night as a teenager in my room listening to Chuck Chillout, DJ Red Alert, and Mr. Magic spin the hottest hip-hop classics. I would sit there in front of my dual tape deck trying to record the songs just right and make sure I would cut out as much of the DJs voice as possible. Now back in those days if a boy were interested in a girl he would make her a tape. Oh yeah, that's how you showed her you liked her (*no kissing!*). Just sit down and record some of your favorite songs for her and if you really, really liked her you would create a slow jam tape. Daddy used to label one side, the Quiet Storm and the other side would say Funky Fresh Dope Mix. I thought I was really doing something. And don't let Yvonne Mobley come on... oh man! Those were the days!

I think some of my most favorite times with the both of you are when we are in the car and we are listening to music. It reminds me of riding in the car with Grandpa when I was little and he would play Sugar Hill Gang, Rapper's Delight. We would both sing along to the rhymes in his burgundy Buick Regal. Today Daddy has an iPod with several playlists on it; one of them is labeled BonsaiDream (*Daddy's nicknames for the two of you*). On that playlist are about 30 songs you all have enjoyed at one time or another. Some you like more than others, and well, some Daddy tolerates more than others. There are some road trips where you will request the same song about 10 times in a row and sing along with the same joy as if you heard it for the first time.

Now I don't know how much you will remember these songs when you get older so I am going to provide you a small playlist of some of your most requested songs at the age of 6 and 4. Just a little reminder of the songs you love.

So, as promised on every 10th day... here is your list, your 'BonsaiDream Most Requested' PLAY list from back in *your* day.

1. *Fight Song* - Rachel Platten
2. *Tightrope* -Janelle Monae
3. *Girl on Fire* - Alicia Keys
4. *Rainbow Connection* - Muppets
5. *Wanna Be Startin' Something* –Michael Jackson
6. *Jam On It* -Newcleus
7. *Nuttin' But Love* -Heavy D & the Boyz
8. *Daughters* -John Mayer
9. *Isn't She Lovely* –Stevie Wonder
10. *God Only Knows* – Beach Boys

MORAL – Sometimes you just have to drop the windows and turn the music all the way up.

⚬

40 days, 40 years, 40 life lessons – Day 31

Dear Basil and Sabine,

I mentioned to you earlier that we would talk more about trust – the meaning of trust, the value of trust. Right now you hear mommy and daddy ask you to tell us the truth whenever we sense that something may be wrong or if something happened at school. We want you to know that we expect you to give us what really happened in any given situation. How many cookies did you eat already? Why are your socks wet? Who put the remote in the fireplace? It's the truth we want, and we *can* handle it.

When daddy was younger I was caught pulling the leaves off of Grandmama's houseplants. I had been pulling off the leaves closest to the floor and blaming it on Uncle Dwayne since he could only crawl, until one day she caught me in the act. I was punished for doing the deed *and* for lying about it in the first place. As I got older there would be more times that I was caught telling white lies to Grandmama and Grandpa and each time I did so I was punished accordingly. What I did not realize is that I was not simply lying; I was also eroding their trust in me. If I could not be upfront and truthful with them, then how could they trust me with things like, keys to the car or keys to the house? They would have to wonder if I was going to always be honest with them, if I could be trusted to do the right thing. **Bottom Line** – could they trust their son?

Looking back now, I believe Grandmama and Grandpa could actually tell when I wasn't being truthful with them. I think that on several occasions they wanted to see just how far I was willing to let the lie go on before I got so wrapped up in it I didn't know if I was coming or going. You see lying is a zero sum game. You never truly win with lying. Even if you feel like you pulled one over on someone you are *always* going to have to live with the guilt of not being completely honest. Over time that dishonesty will chip away at you and leave you feeling quite horrible in-side, always wondering if you are going to get caught. I know; I have had plenty of practice. I lied so frequently it began to become somewhat of a second language for me. And over the course of time the reality is that I lost friends and people I cared for because they could no longer trust me. I had eroded enough trust in my relationships that people were not willing to allow me 2nd, 3rd, and 4th chances to make up for the lies I told. And why should they? These are the consequences of your actions, *my* actions. And once you no longer hold someone's trust, it is nearly im-possible to gain it back. No matter how hard you wish it weren't so. And girls, that is a hard pill to swallow.

Listen to me very carefully. There is nothing so bad out there in the world that you should feel you have to lie to those you love or make up stories to cover up something you may have done wrong. The mark of courage is in owning up to our faults and taking responsibility for the mistakes we have made. And while it may not seem very easy to do so in the beginning, believe me when I say it is 1000x easier to deal with telling the truth than it is to face someone who no longer trusts you – especially those you love.

MORAL – Every mirror reflects the lies you hold onto… Trust Me.

∝

40 days, 40 years, 40 life lessons –
Day 32

Dear Basil and Sabine,

Typically when I sit down to write you these letters it is either quite late at night or very early in the morning. And most of the time I have a fairly good idea of what I am going to say to you. However, there have been times where I begin to write and I actually have to just let the words sort of come to me from one sentence to the next. If it seems like on some days the subject of the lesson is somewhat loosely put together, have no fear, I am fairly confident about wrapping things up by the end of the letter. Such is the fact today.

You see I went to sleep last night filled with worry and angst. I couldn't slow my head down to think straight and every time I began to write you a letter, I found myself drifting off topic toward something extremely irrelevant. By the time I woke up, got in the car and found myself crossing the 14th street Bridge, I realized I hadn't gotten any closer to providing you with a suitable lesson. And then I realized something that has happened a few times before during this journey. You see, some of these letters, these lessons, are just as much for me as they are for you and I should be more accepting of this fact. You see Daddy still needs lessons too.

American comedic philosopher Sir Christopher Rock once stated that the only job a father has is to keep his daughter off the pole. Now while I don't necessarily disagree with philosopher Rock, I take exception with this being the *only* job a father has with relation to his daughter(s) preparedness for life. I will be sure to talk at length with him about this the next time the two of us share a conversation. Now I do believe Mr. Rock was speaking somewhat in jest (*I mean hello, he IS a paid jester*). I happen to believe he is quite an adoring father of his two daughters. But if I do get the opportunity to speak with Mr. Rock I would like to talk with him about so much more than the pole scenario.

I want to talk with him about your happiness throughout the course of your life. How fathers raise our daughters to be happy with themselves, happy in their spirit and happy in thought as it propels them day to day. This is what gives me pause or worry as it did last night. You see with these letters it is my hope that you will be able to take away something that will make a difference to you as you grow. I want you to look at the mistakes I have made, look at the lessons I have learned and try to steer clear of my potholes. But I often get bogged down and concerned too much about the potholes you *are* going to hit and asking myself have I done enough or *will* I do enough to prepare you for what lay in the road ahead. While I am confident that both your mother and

I are doing what we can to expose you to as much opportunity and education as we possibly can I still ask myself quite frequently is it enough? Is it enough to keep you above the fray? Is it enough to ensure your happiness?

When I finally come back down from that plateau of worry and angst I come away with several things (*headache aside*). One, I try to repeat the mantra that all I have is today. That's it. To worry about tomorrow and when I will have time to get the groceries this weekend is fruitless. It may be part of the human condition to want to think past the moment; however I need only concern myself with what I am able to wrap my arms around today. I struggle with this notion. I really do. I want so much to control how the story will unfold for you both, for me, for our family. But it just doesn't work that way. The sooner I can accept this, I know the happier in fact I will be. As such, I have begun to see more clearly that there is a direct correlation drawn from the happiness in my own life which will then be directed to the happiness in yours. My wish is for each of you to have a life fulfilled. A life where you are successful, self-loved and happy with yourselves -- and I understand more so now that I have reached the end of the letter that I need not worry about whether the wish will come true, but instead simply be a role in your success today, be the one that loves you today and be happy for and with you today.

MORAL – Your Great grandfather was right, "Worry is interest paid on taxes that never come due."

༖

40 days, 40 years, 40 life lessons –
Day 33

Dear Basil and Sabine,

The summer before I left for college I wanted to take my family out for a special dinner. I felt like showing them a proper thank you for the first 18 years of supporting (**read:** *tolerating*) me. Though that wasn't all; I also wanted to be sure to impress them with my choice of restaurant and show I could spread around the money. I selected the Bird and Bottle Inn in Garrison, New York just off of Route 9. By all means feel free to Google it (Google should still be around when you read this). We had always passed this restaurant on the way to see my Grandparents and it always seemed like an intriguing location, I was curious what was behind its alluring oval sign with the pheasant upon it. I had worked hard that summer landscaping and saved up money toward my first semester of college. But I wanted to dip into a piece of the stash and spread a little around for a nice evening out with loved ones.

I remember it quite clearly. I looked up the number in the yellow pages (*no internet back then*), called the number and made a reservation for five people. I made a family announcement and stated my intentions to take everyone out for dinner. All on me! They were going to be so impressed. We got all dressed up in our dinner attire and headed toward the restaurant. I was so excited; this was going to be a great night. We arrived at the restaurant and were imme-diately seated. I would say the atmosphere is best described as cozy -- Very few tables, dimly lit, with hushed conversation from several couples who were already dining. Our group of five took our seats at the table.

Our waiter came over and went through the standard overtures; welcome, here are your menus, please listen to our specials, can I bring you something to drink, bottle of wine for the table perhaps? It was all like I had envisioned. And mmmmm, look at that fresh bread. Nice. OK, let me go ahead and open this menu here and see what we are working with. Oh Sweet Baby Jesus! Are you kidding me?! Dad, is the car close by? I'm feeling a little weak about the sternum region; must have been something in the $20 tap water. Girls, my eyes as if by second nature went straight to the price side of the menu. Now I made a good wage with Bill Neave Landscaping, but I just wasn't ready to part with it all in one night. And then my eyes moved over to the actual food. Well look, I took Latin all through high school and I still couldn't decipher what they were offering at the ole B&B Waldorf Astoria that night! With my stomach in knots I watched my family carefully ma-neuver through that menu and then place their dinner orders, hoping everyone would somehow find the bread more than filling. I could feel a twinge of awkwardness at the table as my family was never one to truly mince words. And I think they held out as long as they could just to make me feel better. But the only one truly digging the ambience and the food was Grandmama. I think everyone at the table either wanted the waiter to bring out more bread or have Grandpa drive us back to the Denny's we passed on the way down. But we soldiered through.

By the time dinner was finished and the check came daddy had sweated through his Gordon Gartrell (*Denise made one for me too...*). I swallowed hard and opened the little book the waiter kindly placed in front of me as if I asked him to do it when we first sat down -- The memory on this guy. I tried not to let the overwhelming feeling of grief show on my face, but my parents could see right through me. Grandpa asked if I needed any help. I looked at him as steady as I could, attempting valiantly to show my best face as I assured him that I had it covered. Lucky for me I wanted to feel like a big shot by carrying a lot of cash on me -- cash that was supposed to be meant for my first semester of college. But, I did what I set out to do; I took my family out to dinner. Though I don't think I impressed anyone at the table that night and it's no fun driving home broke and hungry.

Basil and Sabine, I have too many Bird & Bottle Inn stories to count, some a whole heck of a lot worse too. Spending money I didn't have to impress people I don't need to. It's a horrible vice. Thinking you can gain favor with people by spending money on them is only good for one thing – sending you home with less money and no more real friends than you had before the menu got to the table. If you go through life trying to impress people through money in your pocket or portraying a person other than who you truly are, you are likely to discover that whatever it is you seek is not truly worth much of anything. Family and true friends need not have a dollar amount attached to them, their love and admiration of you is free.

MORAL – Gallon of gas in 1991 to travel to Bird & Bottle Inn - $1.01; Bird & Bottle Inn tab - $alot.99! A dinner with family I can laugh about forever – Priceless.

♣

40 days, 40 years, 40 life lessons – Day 34

Dear Basil and Sabine,

When I started writing these letters to you, Grandpa wrote me a small note and talked about what the course of this journey would begin to feel like as the days passed on. I also spoke with David Stewart one of daddy's college roommates who inspired this idea in the first place and he expressed to me the emotions I would feel as I got closer to the end. I am starting to understand now what each of them meant as some of these topics become a bit more personal. It was my intent that you might actually find some of these lessons rather comical, but I find that if I am truly being forthright in giving you something you can truly use throughout your life some of these will not always be funny.

I don't have a story to tell you with this letter; it is meant more so as something for you to keep mindful of as you grow older. When I watch the two of you now I see that in your interactions with family and with friends you are quite loving and friendly in your dispositions. It is my hope that within your hearts you stay this way, that you continue to hold a peacefulness about you as you grow. There are going to be times when you will have to deal with raw emotion, specifically the emotion of anger. With this you will have to be very careful. As I look back over the course of my life and think about the times I have let anger dictate my actions or reaction, I find that the results were never quite positive. In fact many of them are quite cringe-worthy. Out of anger I once kicked a metal garbage can across an office breaking a television. Out of anger I once put my fist through a laptop screen. Out of anger I have yelled things from behind the wheel of my car that have left me looking at myself in the rearview mirror, asking 'who *are* you?'

You should each have a healthy understanding that perhaps the most debilitating thing you can do to yourself is hold onto anger. Don't let anger or hate linger in your heart and mind. Anger can begin to consume you and if you do not let it go you will find that your life is less fulfilling and you keep yourself from moving forward productively. There have been too many times in my own life where the decisions I have made based on anger have left me holding the short end of the stick, wondering how did I get here? You can truly wind up hurting yourself in the long run when the choices you make in life are led by anger.

I wish I could provide you with a magic formula for how you deal with the emotion of anger. The truth of the matter is you are going to have to do your best to take a full account of the situation and understand where your anger is coming from. If you can address the source of the emotion you are a good portion of the way there. The rest of the equation is perhaps the most difficult and that is the letting go. I have been told on many occasions that I am the one responsible for any anger I allow inside of me and as such I am the sole entity who can rid myself of that feeling. I admit that perhaps the hardest part is actually accepting responsibility for what may have caused the anger in the first place. And that is a hard truth.

MORAL – Call Oprah, I just had my aha! moment.

♋

40 days, 40 years, 40 life lessons – Day 35

Dear Basil and Sabine,

At some point in your life I expect that you might ask me my thoughts on love. I hope it is after you turn 30. Right now, before you go to sleep at night I always say I love you. Whenever I am about to leave you, I always say

I love you. I get a smile on my face whenever I hear either of you say 'I love you too.' And I often wonder what love means for you inside those little hearts and minds of yours. I think about your understanding of love and how love grows as you grow. I will admit that Daddy still hasn't really gotten a good grasp on love. What I mean is -- I am still trying to understand how sacred love is and how it should be respected and cherished. I regrettably don't always treat love how it should be treated. But I do know that I love my family, I love you both dearly, I will always love and respect your mother and I love my friends. I need to do better at expressing love and showing love beyond just the words. As I have grown I come to find that love can take on many different meanings; it is used in varying context amongst people depending on whom and what they are talking about. We often think of love as it pertains to a fairytale or romance novel. There actually used to be a television show called the Love Boat - come aboard, they're expecting you... I digress.

What daddy is about to tell you may shock you a bit and I actually laugh a little at myself as I came to the revelation. I have never said this before to either of these individuals but I feel they should know. I love Uncle Rock and Uncle Will. Rahman Branch and William Edward Monden, Jr. are two of daddy's closest friends and I trust them with my life and I trust them with the safety and care of my family, meaning you. I have known each of them for more than half of my life and I have grown to respect, care, admire and yes, love them. I love them for the men they have become. I love them for the husbands they have become. I love them for the fathers they have become. Each of them has seen me at my lowest point and stood by me even when I was in the wrong, ensuring their outstretched arms were there to lift me up. I cannot begin to tell you how many times I have needed their support and they were right there to provide it, whether it is an ear to listen or kind word to help my spirit. In this day and age there are some that will hear this and mock such a thought, but I have no issue with saying that I love them both.

Your Uncle Rock has stood up for me far too many times for me to count. When I was even dead wrong he vehemently went to bat for me and never denounced our friendship. For this I will be eternally grateful. Uncle Rock went from being the first person I met at UVa to standing as my Best Man at my wedding and I trust our brotherhood will last a lifetime. Quite recently I had the pleasure of sitting and talking with Uncle Rock covering just about everything under the sun. In the midst of the conversation on the porch there were moments of silence where nothing was said, but in those moments I was happy to be able to be there with him, my friend. As we get older these moments become less and less frequent as family and other life commitments take priority, so when you can share time with a friend, it means that much more to you.

Your Uncle Will and I have history that could fit 40 more letters to you. I will let you in on a little secret. Actually, ask your Uncle Will about the convenient store across from our High School and what it has to do with him getting into college. He will enjoy telling you *that* story. Your Uncle Will and I have shared some dynamite life moments together. I was able to see him graduate from Morehouse College. We were both in the Navy together. We even slept in a car outside of Frankie Cutlass' Bronx apartment just to be sure we were on Hot 97 (*bonding moments, every one*). I think perhaps the one thing I admire most about Uncle Will is the incredible father he is to Justin, Josh, and Kyleigh. He goes to great length not to miss a practice, game, or kitchen playdate and when he can't make it, he knows he has the support of an incredible bride to play both roles while he is gone several states away ensuring his family is taken care of. When I see Uncle Will behind the wheel of a Honda minivan it makes me smile, because I remember a time when we wouldn't be caught dead in something like that, but he makes it look as cool as the other side of the pillow.

I know we will have an opportunity to talk further about love in your life as you both get older, but I needed to start the conversation with you about love that I know is true, about love that I understand. Love has no gender, it has no color, and it has no physical make up. Love is present in our hearts. It is how we talk and more importantly how we function around those we pronounce as loved ones. As men, we tend to shy away from conversations of love. I believe we too frequently bend to the stigma of society on this one. This is something I hope you never come to bear witness. I hope you both are able to fight such stigma and ignorance. Men can love one another. We should do more of it honestly. Men tend to look too aggressively upon one another, always trying to measure each other's manhood based on our ability to beat the other one down. Uncle Will and Uncle Rock are strong men if for no other reason than that they are husbands and fathers who support and **love** their families. End of story.

MORAL – Love from within.

ဝှ

40 days, 40 years, 40 life lessons – Day 36

Dear Basil and Sabine,

As you both get older you will begin to gain an appreciation for the term, reputation. It will take on different meaning as you move through high school, college and then onto your professional careers and family life, but rest assured maintaining a polished and respected reputation is something I strongly advise you strive for. Reputation starts with character and self-respect. Do you have it? Now I don't mean, being a character. I nailed that one down pretty good for the both of you. What I mean is, are you an individual who carries themselves in such a way that you are always striving to be the highest common denominator through any given situation. Do you possess the innate quality of good character? In your early years your reputation is woven from the family of which you are born. How people perceive your parents generally sets the expectation of how they determine your ability to act right.

A term I heard frequently as a child was, "I know your mother taught you better than that." And 10 out of 10 times they were usually right. But as time unfolds and you find yourself disengaged from the nest (because you *will* disengage), you are going to begin to establish your own reputation, based on **your** own actions. Basil and Sabine Mann are going to be separate individuals who one day step out and make their mark on the world. It is going to be up to you to further set the foundation for how your reputation is going to be built. Your self-respect plays a large role in this.

When Daddy left for college at 18, I was a young, confident, courteous young man. But I was also quite selfish. I have made mention of this to you before, that often times my own selfishness, my predilection to think about Bashon Mann in front of all else has cost me friendships and precious relationships. When you establish a habit of acting in such a fashion, well, this contributes to your reputation. I showed lack of character. I have discovered now at 39 and nearly 12/12ths that character perceptions I set at the age of 19 and 20 have become and indictment on how I am viewed today, nearly 20 years later. You have to consider that in most all cases you *only* get one chance to make a first impression. And some people have incredible memories.

I want you to think about what I am telling you and apply it to most all aspects of your life and the choices you will make as you get older. Whether to pick up the cigarette because you see others doing it, whether to stay out late past the curfew your parents have set for you, or whether to do what you know is unlawful because you think it will make you cool. Make no mistake these will potentially be costly decisions and you never know if one poor decision will adversely affect you many years down the road. Poor decision-making truly isn't a habitual course of action I would recommend.

If you are reading between the lines of this letter, good, it means your mother and I have done our job. I can now talk to Mr. Chris Rock and tell him of our success. You may one day lament that you live under a roof with rules and established order. Know that it is not only for the sanity of the elders in the room but also for your protection and well-being. However, take heart in the fact that you will soon be granted parole for good behavior and with a warm hug and an invitation for a welcome return you will find yourself out amongst the world, ready to show them what courageous, scholarly young women are capable of and that you will do so with verve, tenacity, style, and good character. Your investors are counting on you.

MORAL – If you know better, do better.

℅

40 days, 40 years, 40 life lessons – Day 37

Dear Basil and Sabine,

Your mother is Dr. Anika M. Simpson of Cleveland, Ohio - a Spelman woman. I met her in August of 1999 in Memphis, Tenn. If you ask her about the peephole saga at her apartment door on the day we first met, her story will differ from mine. But she opened the door and her smile made me smile. She is intelligent, beautiful, and full of wonder – all of the things I see in the both of you. Your mother is something very special. She gave all of herself to her family and she made a nurturing home for her family. Your mother loves you unabashedly and with every fiber of her being. Remember this.

On March 5, 2007 and November 19, 2008 you two glorious gifts from God came into our world and made everything in our lives **better** and you still do every second of every day. I watched your mother carry you inside of her; I watched her labor with you and I watched her deliver you amidst unimaginable pain. Basil your epidural only hit half your mother's body and Sabine, well you just wanted out before the anesthesiologist could get the cart in the room. She breastfed you in the dark of night while daddy slept soundly, she rocked you when you cried while daddy slept soundly. She did all of this without complaint. She did this because she is your mother. When daddy went away on those big Navy ships it was mommy that potty-trained you; when daddy went to help people in other countries it was mommy that dressed you for school, picked you up and fed you dinner before putting you to sleep at night. And when daddy went to Afghanistan mommy had to do all those things alone, day after day after day, and you know what? – she didn't complain. She did it because she is your mother.

If ever you feel the urge as you get older to question your mother's decisions or have the audacity to talk back to her or heaven forbid stop talking to her in your teenage years because she wouldn't let you wear makeup or have a cellphone, we are going to sit down and have a talk, a long one. And I am going to pull this letter out and make *you* read it over and over and over again until you understand the sacrifice your mother has made for you. Until you understand the difficult decisions she had to make in order for her to provide you with the best possible representation of a strong woman and mother she could be for you, so that you could look at her and say, that is the woman I want to become, that is the woman I admire.

I know that right now there are things your young minds cannot always comprehend, but it remains our responsibility to keep you focused on being as happy and productive as you can possibly be. I want you to know that when you are older we will have longer, honest discussions about life and the peaks and valleys associated with it. I will be here to answer your questions honestly. Life rarely unfolds as you may have first imagined it would and that is as true as the day is long, but life will go on. The joy is in waking up, even in times when you feel you cannot and taking those first steps of wherever your journey is to take you. Your mother's courage is a symbol of that joy. A joy in knowing who **you** truly are and what it means to love **there** first before allowing any other love in and she wants that for you. Be ever mindful of your mother's heart Basil and Sabine, because she holds you both inside of it. I ask you as your father, always **love** her FULLY.

MORAL – Your mother gave you your life; respect hers.

40 days, 40 years, 40 life lessons -
Day 38

Dear Basil and Sabine,

I need a small favor from you. I promised you that I would write you 40 letters, but I need to use one of your letters to write to Grandmama. I need to tell her something that I have waited too long to say. I will make it up to you if you would allow me to use this letter for her, ok?

Dear Mom,

I have been writing letters to your granddaughters so that they would have something from me that showed how life is full of lessons. I wanted these lessons to serve as a roadmap so they would perhaps learn from some of the mistakes I made along my path. Over the course of writing the letters I inadvertently took myself on a bit of a journey. It became somewhat therapeutic each day to relay my memories and feelings to them. I was able to open up my heart and give them pieces of me that were true. Pieces I didn't always know I had within me quite honestly. As with other challenging times in my life, times I am certain you remember well, I had to reach back to find Bashon again - as I found myself careening off the rails of life, looking for some steady ground to stand on. You and I have spent the last few years talking quite a bit about the issues in my life, and you once again stood me up, held my hand, wiped my tears and told me everything was going to be alright. It seems that even as I get older *that* sequence tends to remain the same as it did when I was 3.

Mom, I am writing this letter to you today so Basil and Sabine can know exactly how I feel about you. I want them to know the tremendous blessing you have been in my life. Quite a long time has passed since I took a moment to sit down and tell you a few things that were on my mind through a letter. I think you will remember I used to do this quite frequently when I was younger, especially when I needed to apologize for my antics. Remember the laundry basket full of pricey unmentionables and the ink pen incident? "Dear Mom, here's some money that I can spare for your damaged underwear!" I hope you can laugh about that now. Nevertheless, I wanted to tell you in no uncertain terms all that you mean to me. So I figured before I get any closer to 40 I should put pen to pad (*fingers to keyboard*) and tell you what has been on my mind.

You see Mom, after all of these years I have finally reached a point in my life where I am ready to look forward and leave the worst parts of my life behind me. I need to do this now before it is too late. I have grown tired of clinging to the memories of wrong turns throughout my life and the time I have wasted of those who have loved and cared for me. I know it is time to become my own change agent. I know *you* are tired. I know Dad is tired. I know you have done all that you possibly can to support me and my family and I know you have sacrificed precious time and gifts in your own life to ensure I had the things to keep me on my feet. And I am aware there have been times when I took this for granted. I have not always shown my appreciation for your sacrifice, but believe me when I tell you, for this I will be forever grateful.

Mom, this was the letter that was always going to be the hardest one to write and I knew it from the beginning. I put it off as long as I could because I feared I could never accurately express to you what you have meant in my life. I have a fear I will never be able to show you the proper return for all you have invested. And while I know in your heart you have **no** expectation of payment, there *is* an expectation of love. And I want you to know that in these letters to Basil and Sabine I am giving all the love you gave to me right back to them. This is my 'Pay It Forward.' And it came from a genuine place Mom. It came in ways that I often did not realize what happened until after it was done. That's how I know it was real.

Mom, you have talked with me most all of my adult life about how God will come and find a way into my life when I need God most. You were right. I know that you already probably know the moment I found myself down on my knees asking God to please take my burdens from me. And there I was, not having been inside of a church since I could remember and in possibly my worst hour I found myself on my knees crying out for help. I called you and asked that you pray with me over the phone and you did. Second by second, hour by hour I am moving forward with God in my life.

Mom, please don't ever leave my side. I need you now in my life more than ever before. I need your guidance, your wisdom, and I need your understanding. I need to know I am raising your granddaughters to be the fantastic young women they are meant to be. I need to know I am being a good father. But Mom, you should also know that even with those needs, I accept the responsibility of standing as a man and as a father to my children who now **need** me as I needed you. There was a time when I knew you would always be there to catch me fall, that you would be present to fix what I broke. I counted on it. I grew to depend on it. And one day I turned away from it, thinking I had everything I needed to answer it all on my own. And here I am telling you now, there are days when I just need to hear your voice and tell me that it's going to be alright. Tell me that it's all happening the way it should.

Mom, there is a children's book I read to the girls from time to time right before bedtime called, 'Love You Forever' that describes the growth of a young boy and his mother. The repeated verse of the book goes, "I'll love you forever, I'll like you for always, As long as I'm living my baby you'll be." But toward the end of the book when the son is old enough to hold his own mother in his arms, it is the son who sings the verse and repeats, 'As long as I'm living my mommy you'll be.' Mom, the first time I read this book to Basil and Sabine I could barely see the last few pages as my eyes filled with water. I had never read the book before and was not expecting the overwhelming feeling I had once I reached the end of the book. Kind of like right now quite honestly.

Linda Melton Mann, my mother who gave me life, You taught me to stand tall, you pushed me forward, you put **us** first when I know it wasn't easy, but your heart was filled with God's love and you knew that we needed you each and every day. I can't tell you how much love I have for you Mom. And I just need you to hear it from me today. I need my girls to know. And Basil and Sabine, when I end conversations, letters, and emails to Grandmama our tradition has always been to say that I love you hotdogs and ice cream, it simply means that I love her as much as my favorite things in life. And so now when I end my letters to you they will end with your favorite things.

Love hotdogs and ice cream,

Your son, Bashon

MORAL – I'll Always Love My Momma, She's my favorite girl.

☙

40 days, 40 years, 40 life lessons – Day 39

Dear Basil and Sabine,

You both make me laugh, you really do. I am sitting in my room trying to write you this letter and all I hear is you both talking yourselves silly with about 101 dolls and stuffed animals on the top bunk. I've tried to write this first paragraph 17 times already, but I keep laughing to myself. Pretty soon I am about to quote a Samuel L. Jackson bedtime story. (All the cool parents know what I mean… *Go the F@ck to Sleep!*)

But seriously, the morning is fast approaching and so is the end of this 40 day road we've been on. I will be honest with you little ladies, I really didn't know what these letters were going to become after I wrote the first one. I hope in the end you will have gained something from what I have shared with you. My wish for you is that one day when you look back on the totality of the life you've lived; you can do so with great satisfaction and peace of mind. And if in fact you did live fully, then the pictures that flash across your mind will tell a wonderful story. For each and every one of us has a story. Short ones, long ones, funny ones, inspiring ones, sad ones, and even those stories that seem to stop and then start again in a new direction – and I'd like to think they all would make for interesting reading. Try to remember that you can learn something from most anyone and at any time. This is what makes us all intricately special and delightfully human. We are all walking around living and trying to make the most of the life we were given.

My suggestion to you and know it is only a suggestion, as I expect you to live *your* own life, would be to seek adventure but be safe in your endeavor as life is also fragile. Care for it. Think with passion and dream *a lot*; for there is no wrong in dreaming, only limitless wonder and potential for greater actuality. Don't spend too much time on regret; while life may certainly possess them you do not have to burden yourself with past misgivings, this is something you *can* control. Remember that the incredible tool which exists between your ears can also be used to great detriment if you do not treat it wisely. Be mindful of allowing sadness, misery and negativity to roam inside there, too much of this concoction can be habit forming and soon your modus operandi will have you on a hamster wheel rather than the path less travelled.

Girls, there are going to be pieces of your life that will leave you completely breathless and while there will be times along your flight path that will bring hiccups and potholes, know that you will experience moments of extreme joy which will help propel you much higher as you continue to fly. This is life. Embrace it all and be your best possible friend. Love your flaws wholly and know that is part and parcel of what makes you who you are. There is no shame in this. While we are not perfect beings, we can be perfect in our being. And know you are each perfectly and beautifully made from God's love. This I know to be true.

I do not know what tomorrow brings, but I know I am blessed with today and so my story and your story continue unfolding as it should. The first 40 years of pictures have long been floating through my mind providing a multi-layered narrative, but I am anxious to see these new chapters, these new pages have you both inside them and I want to read the stories **WE** write together. I have a feeling they will be bestsellers.

MORAL – Live your dreams; make them your story and share it with those you love.

ᑯᒧ

40 days, 40 years, 40 life lessons –
Day 40

Dear Basil and Sabine,

It's August 10th. There was a time when just thinking about the pending arrival of this day would send me into a euphoric daze. Something about your birthday just makes your whole spirit feel good. At least that's the way it was for me as a child. Over the years however I have come to learn an important lesson about birthdays and expectations – they don't mix. Well into my adult years at the onset of my birthday I would anticipate a multitude of birthday wishes, gifts, and huge parties from people to whom I offered nothing quite as near in return. When none of these anticipated items came to fruition I would sit disappointed and frustrated that my birthday never quite measured up to my immature thought pattern.

I remember my 13th birthday when my parents took us to Busch Gardens and toward the end of an otherwise exciting, expensive, and adventurous day, Grandmama asked me why I looked like I wasn't having a good time as we walked toward the car. I told her I thought I would have kissed a girl by the time I was 13. Grandmama chuckled at such a silly thought. Why couldn't I simply enjoy the gift of an amusement park? (Listen up, Daddy's first kiss did eventually come along and I am glad I wasn't 13; nor was she by the way!)

By the time daddy became an adult I began to spend many of my birthdays either alone or away from family, often wondering why I was never as happy as I wanted to be on that actual day. I will be honest with you girls, by the time I became a father and you both were small I still sought to spend my birthday's alone; always convincing myself that my own birthday expectations could never be met by any friends or loved ones. I selfishly created a false expectation and placed it on people who cared about me, believing I deserved some personal grand overtures when I had done nothing to receive such.

What I eventually found over time was as you distance yourself from loved ones and friends, ultimately losing them from your life completely, you discover a clear realization of what you needed before they went away. I didn't need to spend those birthdays alone; I needed to be around family. I should have been around family. That's worth celebrating. Family and friends are what make a birthday happy. I'll take that gift any day I can.

Basil and Sabine, as promised, it is a 10th day and I owe you one final list. So here it is:

The "10 things Daddy needs you to know" –

1. I need you to know that I am sorry for not being with you each and every day.
2. I need you to know that I will always work hard to ensure you don't want for anything.
3. I need you to know that I will never turn away from you.
4. I need you to know that any pain you feel, I feel alongside with you.
5. I need you to know that when you need to talk with me I will always be there to listen.
6. I need you to know that I strive every day to be a better daddy for you.
7. I need you to know that your smiles will always dry my tears.
8. I need you to know that driving you both home from the hospital was the slowest I have ever driven a car in my life.
9. I need you to know that the love I have for you in my heart stretches beyond the moon and stars.
10. I need you to know that you will always be my little girls. Please stay this way forever.

MORAL – You will always be my greatest gifts!

ℐ

41 days, 40 years, 41 life lessons – Day 41 (BONUS)

Dear Basil and Sabine,

Like McDonald's french fries at the bottom of the bag, everyone likes a little extra! You see, I told you I would make up for that one letter. It dawned on me that I wrote those letters to you about my time at UVa, but I never let you know about how I finished college. Well, remember when I told you how I went down Millington, TN and decided one day to go back to college? It turns out after 3 years down there I graduated from the University of Memphis on December 15, 2001 with a Bachelors of Arts degree, majoring in journalism. That's right, Bashon Mann, college graduate at 28 years old. That's how it went for me. And when it came time for daddy to receive his degree the whole family showed up to the Pyramid in Memphis, Tennessee to witness it for themselves; making me the happiest graduate in the place.

Now the featured speaker for graduation was the Mayor of Memphis, a man by the name of Willie Herenton and I had no intention of listening to what he had to say that day. So, I asked a man I had a very close relationship with, someone who I knew had a penchant for oratory skills, if he would write me a personal commencement address – an address I could read while the Mayor spoke about whatever he was going to. Grandpa was more than willing and BOY did he deliver. Grandpa handed me a folder before the ceremonies and I kept it with me inside of my graduation robe. As the Mayor stood at the podium to give his remarks, I pulled out the folder, opened it and lowered my head to begin reading:

Professors, administrators, friends, family, esteemed graduates; we are gathered here today to celebrate the fruits of your labors. Having diligently followed the regimens of countless teachers, professors and advisors, you have succeeded in meeting the standard by which this University confers its degree. The next step is to re-evaluate YOUR standard and continue your learning accordingly.

Learning is a lifelong activity. To make it any less is to deprive ourselves of an ever-enriching existence. Some of us are visual learners while others are audio learners. It is not the style of learning which matters most, it is a matter of how long we take to acknowledge our own personal style and make the necessary adjustments. Be aware the adjustment may not always be to our strength, but the adjustment must be made to accommodate our advantage. If we refuse to adjust to bring us an advantage, our battle to learn increases; not due to the difficulty of the unlearned material, but to our own refusal to let it be simpler.

Moving on from a graduation ceremony can be intimidating to some, a great source of strength for others. First you must recognize the threshold you have achieved. You are now a graduate of a school of higher learning. So do you seek higher learning based on the skills and aptitudes you have gained, or do you rest on the laurels achieved? Is a thirst for more gained from attaining skills, or is there a contentment which comes with achievement? This is a part of the recognition of learning styles, for while the method may be audio or visual, the quantity of learning refers to neither. The quantity one wishes to learn is based on an inner drive, or motivation. We cannot have all the things we want, so we must decide which things are important to us. It is these things which we shall pursue with the most energy. All the while one should remember, of all the things in the world, it is the *things* which matter least.

Having armed oneself with a diploma from an institution of higher learning, you are not assured of success in life, but you are assured of having the tools to be productive in society. You have established a baseline for your ability to be exposed to new information, ingest the information and then create something from said information. You can create something new; you can revise that which has already been created; or you can make something old more efficient and operable in a new environment. Whatever or wherever your thoughts may take you, you have equipped yourself for the journey. Too often the journey is misunderstood, and peoples key on the destination. But the destination never really provides an answer: when your "here" becomes "there" the only thing which has changed is the "t!" For when you get "there," there now becomes your here, and you will seek another "there." But what matters most is the learning you have acquired in going from here to there and how you are going to apply the new learning to your next journey? Learning is not applied to the destination, for the destination is static. The learning is applied to the journey, which is in motion.

And when is the task complete? The task is completed when the individual says they have had enough. The soul and the mind are very fragile parts of the human structure. Knowing and accepting just how fragile they are will arm us against undue harm to these vital parts of our existence. *"DESIDARATA"* should be required reading and understanding.

To read this essay is not enough. It must be read over and over to completely understand how it fits and affects our daily lives. It is important to understand how our individual lives have an effect on those around us. And when we say "around" us, do not be so naïve to think I reference the physical space. There are people who are around you, but are hundreds and thousands of miles away, but feel so very close. Always recognize them, in your daily thoughts and actions. You have attained a higher level of learning, so you have demonstrated your ability to comprehend just who you are and some of what you are capable of doing.

Nothing you do is ever done in a vacuum. Someone is always watching, looking to imitate, duplicate, or replicate what you have done. This should not be a burden to you, but a watchword for future actions. Choose the words you speak carefully, for those words become your habits. Seek and you shall find. There is never a missed opportunity, for someone else will pick up that which you discard. And if you harbor resentment, happiness will dock elsewhere. You have armed yourself with the strongest tool to help you climb the ladder of success, but if you do not use it willfully and wisely, you will have labored in vain. The piece of paper will open doors, but it has no means to the journey through. The journey is one you must make yourself. Congratulations on your current success; just be sure to place the emphasis on success, so current becomes past. Oh, and the definition for success is not how high you are flying, it is how high you bounce from your last failure. Good luck and best wishes always.

Love, Dad (*Grandpa to you*)

Basil and Sabine - you may want to keep this one handy. It continues to speak volumes to me each time I read it. Grandpa has a way with words.

MORAL – It all comes from somewhere…

༄

II

The Love In Between

42

Dear Basil & Sabine,

Politics. It's a multi-faceted word you will grow to begrudge in life, but also come to accept as a part of the daily lexicon. There are the politics of our government, from the global and national level right down to your everyday PTA and Deacon/Deaconess Board at your church; each governing body is shaped by politics and politicking of the individuals therein. You will come to find that what drives politics are the motives by which individual people or groups of people are inclined to move their agendas in a particular direction in order to arrive at a given end state. There is good in this and there is bad. In a healthy system, politics are discussed and used to broaden views and enhance both government and its citizenry. It is a means by which society is strengthened through educated discourse and enacted via enlightened principle to be used for the greater good. However girls, politics often get in the way of what we like to call, 'the more perfect union.' They can get in the way of our best intentions, and even change how we live our lives. They just get in the way.

I don't really like to talk about my political views or expose my politics at every turn. I feel they can get in the way of otherwise worthwhile friendships and work relationships. I keep my political views for the voting booth. I keep my politics aimed in a position for sensible discourse and of value to me and my family. I keep my politics from getting *in the way.*

Mind you, this is just my opinion. Everyone has them and is certainly entitled and encouraged to disagree. After all, value of diversity lay not just in gender or the color of one's skin, but in thought and ideas. This is what lends toward the perfection of the aforementioned union.

Over time you each will develop your own politics. The politics of how you ask for Christmas gifts will eventually turn into the politics of how you ask for the keys to the car and eventually you will navigate the politics of accepting and deleting Facebook friend requests based on, well… their Politics. And I just think that's kind of an unfortunate reality in today's social media culture. It is my hope that by the time you girls are able to take part in our election process you are able to do so without the distracting taste of ineptitude for our system of government, or better yet the people we elect to run it and their seemingly growing capacity to separate, rather than join together. I hope that you are able to sustain a willing faith in a country you call your own; knowing that of all the politics that matter the least to the people who need help the most just don't get **in the way**.

MORAL – It's best to consider everyone as *essential* personnel.

#43

Dear Basil & Sabine,

In your accomplishments be proud, be humble; yet remember to also be encouraged of your efforts reward. This is what you have earned. Through sacrifice, dedication and discipline in said pursuit, whether a spelling test or passing the bar; you ought to find satisfaction in your abilities to withstand the 'test' and rise to the occasion. Be mindful however of the sacrifices of others which helped to propel you forward – this is perhaps most important. Your success did not occur in a vacuum. There are shoulders upon which you stand to see more clearly, to be free of larger obstacles which may have dissuaded you from moving farther down your path. There is a fine line that separates the self-promotion of one's achievement and the acknowledgement of the circumstances which exist in order for you to reach *your* goals and career aspirations. I would ask that you remain mindful of the difference as your father has not always had this respect or appreciation for the distinction.

Girls, military promotions occur quite frequently, though they are earned, not guaranteed. They are an integral piece of the makeup of our armed forces. Men and women achieve rank based on time in service and the degree to which they have exceled in their given rate of profession. That I have arrived at this particular milestone along the path of my career, it is marked by both reflection and tempered elation. You see, this day is special for a variety of reasons but perhaps the greatest reason of all is that it allows me the opportunity to not only share it with the both of you, but also Grandmama & Grandpa in addition to the family and friends who deserve my sincerest gratitude and heartfelt apologies for not saying before – Thank You.

Thank you for being there when I didn't know how far from 'there' I was, Thank You for standing close when I wanted to be so *far*; Thank You for allowing **love** to be elevated in your hearts so much further than the hurt, disappointment, and selfishness my actions may have depicted. Your genuine feelings of love and devotion have made me who I am – capable of staying grounded in faith and centered on the foundation upon which I was molded as a young child who would become a man. I owe you a debt that can never be repaid – I have but to stand up and say that *you* are responsible for my success and I am taking this moment to forever let it be known I would not have reached this point had it not been for your sacrifice, your love, your friendship, your forgiveness.

Basil and Sabine, you stand to attain many of your own accomplishments throughout your lifetime, this I know to be true. They will serve as a tribute to your dedicated, dogged pursuit of excellence in any course of endeavor you choose. And should you choose to accept these milestones under the quiet cloak of unassuming praise or acknowledgement from others as is your right – please know we, as your family, will still be quite proud and want to share it with the world. For there are those whose sacrifice is cemented in your achievement and for this we ought to always remember. Trust that *your* sacrifice, without even knowing it was present for me today.

MORAL – Daddy's refrigerator door will always have room for your excellent work, whether spelling test or PhD.

⚘

#44

Father's Day Memories

Dear Basil and Sabine,

I've been blessed with the ability of incredible memory recall. I can somehow manage to remember events from my life with vivid clarity going back to the age of 2 or 3 years old. It's a treasure I hope to retain so long as I have my marbles. One of the greatest things about this sort of photographic memory is being able to reach back and replay the moments in your life that while at first may have seemed mundane, were actually some of the most enriching times of your life.

Sabine, I think you know more than anything that Grandpa really likes ice cream, I mean he *loves* the stuff, who can blame him right? And both you and he seem to have a deep appreciation for apple pie and ice cream, which I find rather uncanny actually. Do you ever wonder why I take you guys to get ice cream after school? Well, because going as far back as Hull Homestead nursery school, whenever Grandpa would pick me up at the end of the day, more times than not we would go and get ice cream. And not just any ice cream, it was Carvel ice cream – It was Carvel or nothing, (well maybe Stewart's, it's an Upstate NY thing!) I can remember climbing into the cab of his '74 Forest Green, Ford F-250 and sitting right there on the front bench seat were Carvel ice cream saucers. These typically came in a plastic case of six, but most days there were only four left when I got in the truck. The reality behind the mystery of the missing two never much mattered so long as there was one for me. I can almost smell the interior of that truck now and Grandpa would reach over and hand me one of those cold beauties and we'd both just ride home eating ice cream saucers before dinner with chocolate wafer stuck in his mustache and mine on my face.

Now much like you both today, I spent a lot of time riding with my Dad, though more so in the back seat of the car. It seemed we were always going somewhere – baseball games, ski trips, family vacations. And little kids get a unique perspective from back there. Everything seems bigger and grander from the back seat. I remember a lot of things from those car rides, but one of the best things was the music Grandpa would play on his tape deck (*you have no clue what that is*). I would get a concert with every ride. My first memories are 70s era R&B hits from the Gap Band and Earth, Wind and Fire - but when Sugar Hill Gang came out with Rapper's Delight, I was old enough to sing right along with Grandpa. So one of the greatest things in the world to me would be the both of us rapping through the song and then look at each other at one part saying, "...and the chicken tastes like wood!" Its why now when you girls ask for your favorite songs to be played on the iPod I enthusiastically agree and can't stop grinning from ear to ear when I hear you both singing the words to the same songs Grandpa and I would listen to. And, I will admit that I have gotten used to singing along with you to Alicia Keys and "This Girl is on Fire" (*yes, even with the windows down*).

Girls, back when I was a young boy there used to be a Public Service Announcement (PSA) that played on TV. It was about the dangers of kids and drugs. You see the PSA showed a father asking his young son where he learned about using drugs and where he had acquired the drug paraphernalia that the father was holding in his hands. As the father continued to ask over and over where and how the son had learned of the horrible practice, the son finally yelled out, "You alright... I learned it by watching you!" Basil and Sabine, Grandpa never used drugs; he used love, hard work and he used ice cream and that's what I learned by watching him. It's a lesson he continues to model today and I won't take my eyes off it.

MORAL – You scream, I scream, **WE ALL SCREAM FOR ICE CREAM!** Happy Father's Day George Mann, the chicken still tastes like wood.

ℭ

#45

Basil and the amazing COLUMBIA dream coat

I must admit to being completely unnerved at the debilitating effect with which my emotions can be moved to a state of extremis over a material possession. On Sunday at approximately 4pm I concluded a round of fall/ winter shopping for the children in my life that would have made most any well-seasoned shopper quite proud. I was pleased with the effort I put in as well as the thoughtfulness with which I allowed for a 7 and 5 year old to disagree with 'Dad-reason' and provide them freedom to choose their own clothing ensembles. I stalked the aisles wisely, I utilized the patience of Job and exercised restraint from bending further than my George Costanza wallet would allow. I did not rush, for football rituals had no priority on this day over the warmth and comfort of these smiling faces. I was Dad in a foreign land, yet I would persevere.

Confident in my retail extravaganza I placed child and cloth inside earthen terrain vehicle of the 3rd degree and maneuvered from the parking lot with the sun on my face, a diminutive smile appearing upon my lips as gleeful sounds emitted from behind me. I DAD, have made happiness.

These brave, feminine warriors would arrive at Inspired Teaching School on Monday ready to learn, ready to be bold in their pursuit of knowledge - ready to head to the playground in a new, black, Columbia fleece as temperatures strangely went from 40 to 75 degrees inside of 24 hours. The 7yr old whom I love so deeply played, she played hard; she is my She-Ra. Though, the rising temps made her warm in the COLUMBIA fleece; she was stifled by its hold. She had to break free of the COLUMBIA fleece, black with C-O-L-U-M-B-I-A stitched above the left breast side of the new coat in white letters, purchased just 24 hours earlier. Ready to unleash her boundless spirit upon chutes and ladders, she would enthusiastically throw the new Columbia black fleece to the ground, no longer caring for its embrace. COLUMBIA gave her, us free. Upon the conclusion of her playground romp, she departed – exhausted from play, spent from her jungle gym dominance - the Brand New, Black Columbia Fleece a faint memory in the distance of grassy plains, no longer a necessary item of interest to this dependent whom I would give my life for.

Day of work over I began my ritual traffic dance, a resemblance of nothing at all peaceful in life. Upon my arrival to gather this delightful duo, whom each carries my blood, the news was delivered. I felt *it* coming. It started from a place in which I dare not venture often. Daily Pentagon trials and reality of life emotional struggles buried just beneath the surface of my being I stood above the lost and found bin. Staring into its abyss, I dove in absent the joy of a Thornton Melon triple lindy. With each and every swing of a flailing arm I became filled with a growing rage - none of these items were the BLACK, COLUMBIA FLEECE purchased a day before. They were other things. They were jackets, shirts, hats, gloves of other loved children – other aimlessly forgotten items of cloth so effortlessly disregarded without the conscientious respect for the potentially crazed authority who had purchased the item just a day prior. I reached the bottom of the bin. Nothing, absolutely nothing. Just a bleak, barren, dark, empty canister staring back at me as if to say in a tense, Gene Wilder played Willy Wonka tone, "**You Lose.**"

And by then it had arrived. It's tumultuous force making its way to the surface all at once. The ear-curdling, soul inducing, man-cry of FUUUUUUUUUUUUUUUUUCCCCCCCCCCKKKKKKKKKKKKKKK that erupted from my mouth in front of children, parents, and YMCA aftercare personnel firmly showcased the pure frustration I had encased inside of me. A woeful, single tear-inducing look now forming upon my daughters face will forever be emblazoned in my mind's eye. It will take an overwhelming abundance of hugs and Daddy-daughter time to push that moment away into the farthest reaches of both our memory banks. All over a black, Columbia fleece lost on the playground at Inspired Teaching School.

MORAL – It's just a coat, there are more precious things in life to lose.

⚘

#46

The Book Bag Chase

Parents, ride with me on this one for a moment – For Moms and Dads who find themselves immersed in what we call, "the Morning Routine" you may just find yourself vehemently shaking your head in agreement with this yarn.

I find that there are no less than 100 different checklists items involved in the Morning Routine. It starts with in fact *you* waking up, getting yourself in a state of tempered serenity before moving forward as you are comfortable to begin checking off everything in between that will eventually lead you to departing the house with a child or children who are essentially clean, dressed, fed, and carrying everything they could possibly need for a full day of school. Items such as lunches, book bags (*pay attention to this*) and soccer gear for practice after school (Yours truly forgot this yesterday) all fall on this checklist.

Now on this particular Friday morning I found myself waking up feeling a bit more determined than usual to get the Mann children to school on time. You see the incredibly wonderful school of learning which these two attend has a particularly strict rule about arriving on time. Anything and I mean anything, walking into that building after 0845 gets a tardy slip. Please understand the military man in me prides myself on making sure the proper, on time arrival of my children is never brought into question at the doorstep of Inspired Teaching School. If I have to nudge other cars or pedestrians to make sure I hit the mark, let there be no mistake I am up to the test. Now all aggression aside, what this means is I have to orchestrate the M.R. like a Marine Corps drill sergeant and if I were to record it, I am sure some of it would sound a bit like Gunny. But it's all said with love and an extra abundance of care and affection, right down to the pink and white bow Sabine demanded in her hair this morning. "Make sure you tie it like you would a shoelace," she patiently demanded. (*As I look into the proverbial camera of life*)

Teeth brushed, check. Clean underwear, check. Hair done, check. Lunches made, check. Nutritious breakfast, check. Coats, shoes, book bags, smiles...Check, Check, Check, Triple Stamp Check, enough, I am good. Let's rock! We are off to battle Phase II. What is Phase II you ask? HaHaHaHaaa (RIP Geoffrey Holder, 7Up never tasted so good!) Why Phase II are these DC streets and the 85% of moronic simpletons who lack the pedigree to operate motor vehicles therein. If I wore a heart-rate monitor during my commute to and from drop-off and pick-up I would without a doubt display signs of impending heart ailment. But alas, I managed to dip, dive, slash, and craft my way to a dynamite parking space all the while trying to ignore the Basil & Sabine iPod playlist that I am slightly ashamed to admit I have playing in my car. I digress, kids out of truck; walked into building, safely in class, all before 0830. "YOU'RE THE BEST ARRRROUUNNNND, NOTHING'S GONNA EVER KEEP YOU DOWN..." The small victory of the on-time drop off. I know I am not alone.

Now, every once and a while, I believe God and my ancestors have a way of dropping a slice of humble pie right into your lap just to keep you on your toes. Today I saw a fellow Dad whom I enjoy speaking with, Clif Durant. Clif and one another Mom were the "Kiss & Go" volunteers of the day. Now if you are not familiar with "Kiss & Go", let me explain. As I understand, K&G is an arrangement whereby parents can drive their kids to the sidewalk in front of the school and have someone politely open the car door, greet you with a nice hello and then ensure your children are brought safely into the school. All the while you send air kisses to your children, mutter something like, "buh bye, I love you" and get back to sending texts and emails as you drive off without hitting someone else's kid on your way to work which you are now late for. Hence, the "I'm on way" text you just sent. Now, I have never been a 'Kiss & Go' volunteer. My schedule has me in the Pentagon before sunrise most days and when I do have the opportunity to orchestrate "Morning Routine" I just try to keep it moving. But today was different. Today I felt compelled to pause for a second, grab the orange volunteer traffic vest and join Clif curbside. I was happy to do so. We make small talk, we greet cars, we fellowship in the brisk air. Ahhh, life stuff.

Dude, get to the pie. Now I like to make a joke here and there and make light of an otherwise awkward or tense situation. **SCENE** – Toyota F4 pulls up, doors open, 2 children spill out. Rather than do the typical greeting and get the kids inside as instructed, B Mann wants to engage in small talk about the car, asking 2 or 3 questions in rapid succession without even waiting for a response. And why no response you ask? Well these 2 grandparents (*I believe*) *do not* speak English. Soooooooooo, I quickly realize the language barrier, bid adieu, close the door and watch them drive off as quickly as possible. I turn, to look at the child who is now with Clif and there are tears pouring down her frosty, rose colored cheeks. Clif asks, "What's wrong?" Now folks, imagine your child's crying, tear-driven response here, "My book bag is still in the carrrrrrrr...." I can still hear the words beyond the tears. This poor girl's world was going to end if she did not get that book bag. In my attempt to be jovial and spirited I had subtly disengaged these people from their Morning Routine, therefore allowing for them to be thrown off kilter just a scousch, forgetting the coveted book bag.

Clif looked at me, I looked at Clif, we both turned our heads toward the corner of Lincoln Rd NE and Douglas St., as this bright yellow Toyota turned left at an amazing rate of speed (*said for effect*). I didn't have a moment to lose. Cue the Chariots of Fire music please... I took off like Tailwind Turner. By the time I arrived at the corner of Lincoln, I could see this Crayola colored beast disappearing in the distance (*40 yards, tops*). Grandma and Grandpa were FREE!!! I checked the traffic pattern in both directions, carefully calculating my pursuit. I hit it. I would simply cut down 2nd street to avoid on rushing cars and cut the fast disappearing elderly duo off at the pass. The wind in my face, I was slicing down the street like a man going for Gold in Barcelona. I WOULD GET THE BOOKBAG FOR THIS POOR GIRL WHOM I DID NOT KNOW. HER LIFE DEPENDED ON THE BOOK BAG I CONJURED AS I HIGH-KNEED IT DOWN THE BLOCK. My breath heavy, heart racing, 1 block, 2 blocks, other parents screaming at the orange streak passing by them in a flash, GO BASH, GO!!!!! Sorry, can't talk now, I. HAVE. TO. GET. HER. BOOK BAGGGGG!!!! At the end of the 4th block, I would meet my fate -- wouldn't you know it... Grandma and Grandpa realized the extra baggage in tow and turned the corner to meet me. Completely out of breath and unable to say a word from my mouth, thine eyes met with Grandpa's as he extended a pink, princess book bag out of the car window and we nodded assuredly, communicating all we needed to in looks, head nods, and dog-like panting.

I jogged, albeit gingerly back to the front of the school to find Clif and other parents consoling this child on the cold steps. As I extended my arm to give the book bag to her she gently grabbed it, placed it on her shoulder and walked into school, her world now normal again. I turned, smiled and shook Clif's hand as we walked to our cars to go to work. That's the routine.

#47

The Check (*made national news*)

Dear "_____,"

First, I offer my apologies. You see I am not sure how I ought to refer to you. The waiter was instructed not to disclose whom you were when I asked to know. But wait, let me back up a little bit and explain myself. "_____," you didn't know this but today was my youngest daughter's birthday. Her name is Sabine, and this beautiful little pack of dynamite and hug muscle turned six today. When we asked her what she wanted to do for her birthday dinner, she said without hesitation, "Mi Rancho!" It has become a bit of a birthday destination ritual for our daughters to visit this restaurant as these little girls have become enamored with their birthday sombrero tradition and fresh from the oven sopaipillas, coated with honey and confectionary sugar. They are hooked. So we now realize that each birthday heretofore will undoubtedly be spent at Mi Rancho in Silver Spring, Maryland. I am guessing "_____," that you are already undoubtedly familiar with the fantastic menu at this establishment.

November 19, 2014 was not an especially peculiar day for any reason, it was rather cold in the nation's capital but other than the usual beltway driven, dog chasing its tail political nuance that occurs here on a daily basis this was simply not unlike any other day as far as I could see. "_____," I suspect you saw it through a completely different lens however, just my hunch. I do want you to know that I walked into that restaurant this evening wearing my Navy service dress uniform because my daughter asked that I dress up for the occasion of her birthday dinner. I was more than happy to oblige. You see, she does not get to see me in uniform very often, and I was proud of her that she would ask to see me in what Daddy goes to work in. After all it is my work that tends to keep me from seeing them as often as I, and *they* would like. However, all other melancholy realities of life put aside, when we walked in Mi Rancho Wednesday night all was good. We were together, we were smiling, and we were ready to celebrate Sabine.

"_____," my parents George and Linda Mann could not make it down from New York for this birthday dinner, though they made sure they were present in spirit. My mother, the saint she is had made sure to reach out to me just days before to tell me she would send a check in the mail to cover the cost of dinner.

"_____," I am 41 yrs old, so when I tell you that I sometimes hang my head a bit when Mom & Dad say they got "it", well you'll just have to understand though tremendously grateful for the blessing of parents with the energy, ability and will to share so lovingly, there is the small sting of humility and a burden I feel I place upon them from time to time. Things have been difficult the past couple of years and it's a longer story than you probably have time for. Thus, you are asking yourself why am I telling you all of this? I'm longwinded, can never tell a short story. You see "_____," it's just that you caught me flat footed. And maybe that was your intent. You don't know my inner personal struggles, and I don't know yours. Perhaps that is how it is meant to be; perhaps that is the blessing inside the blessing - one I shall just have to accept and learn from. That despite heaviness, strife and anguish it is the openness of one's heart that allows for the good to spread, for healing to be felt. It has been hours now and I have not stopped thinking about the profoundness of your actions Wednesday evening. And, I suspect it is going to take me some time to figure out how I shall properly respond. How do I take your action and create an equally compelling and forceful reaction. How do I pay it forward?

After the fulfilling dinner was consumed and dishes cleared from the table, after dessert was served, birthday songs sung, candles blown out, ice cream, and sopaipillas consumed did the waiter lean over my right shoulder ever so gently to speak. "Sir, your check has been taken care of this evening, and thank you for your service." I looked feverishly around the restaurant, scanning each patron for a telling glance. I needed to know who did this – who was kind enough, generous enough, and human enough in this day and age to reach into their pocket and pay for a mother, a father and their two daughters to have a birthday dinner.

The waiter refused to tell me your name "_____," he heeded your instruction and failed to budge. I'll never know who you are. I'll never be able to personally thank you for doing something I may have merely only thought of in passing, something I may have never done on my own accord. Something I could only wish I had the fortitude and bravery to have done a long time ago.

"_____," you don't know a single burden I may carry or what I may have been going through today, nor do I know the travails of your daily journey; but when I reached my car to begin my drive down Georgia Avenue, I fought back tears as I tried to keep myself together and take in your kindness at its root. You presented me with previously unseen hope and faith; you were a blessing tonight and I will not soon forget your overture. I need you to know that I won't block the flow of generosity; I won't halt your abundance of goodness.

Thank you "_____," you are my "friend."

※

#48

Giving Thanks

Dear Basil & Sabine,

Thank FULL.

I am still getting used to spending Thanksgiving without the both of you -- another one of those unfortunate realities of divorce. As I pushed myself through the paces, moving from one distraction to another this holiday weekend, I finally arrived at a place where the picture became a bit clearer for me. Remember a few letters back when I talked to you about the importance of family? Well, let me talk to you a bit about *this* Thanksgiving and family.

On Wednesday night I left DC to head back home in the middle of a winter weather advisory for the 95 corridor (*I figured why not, less traffic*). By the time I pulled in the driveway at 5 Deer Run around 0130 on Thursday morning, guess who was there standing in the garage? Yup, Grandpa, just like always. The big guy just doesn't sleep until all the baby bears get back to the cave. I walked upstairs and there was Grandmama, one eye open, waving from her bed waiting to get that bear hug before she fell asleep. I walked down the long hallway to the room of my youth and fell asleep within 2 minutes. When I awoke 5 hours later, I was immediately engulfed by the familiar smells of Thanksgiving-past as Grandmama would wake very early to put the finishing touches on bountiful dishes, molded from age-old family recipes that were to be consumed later that evening. In that moment, drifting back in my memory bank, laying there in the bed, I smiled. I was home again.

Same as the year before we headed down to see Aunt Sandy and Uncle Bill on West 86th and Columbus. As you already know, just walking into their apartment brings amazement and wonder. A home so rich with our family's heritage strewn about on every wall, bookcase and 'mannmade' cabinetry piece – again, it is home. Uncle Bill, as per usual glued to his constant television news coverage, I had to put on my best PR professional face in order to convince him that the 1 o'clock pm Detroit game was as much a part of the Thanksgiving fabric as Indians and Pilgrims *"allegedly"* sharing pumpkin pie and candied yams. I digress. Aunt Sandy, bless her heart (no really, she just had heart surgery) was in the kitchen alongside Grandmama making sure the table was filled with just about every piece of food you could imagine. It was incredible, just like always. She didn't miss a beat! (Pardon the pun). We sat down for dinner at 4pm, which means I saw *nada* of that Cowboys vs Eagles game. The table conversation was **intense**; as I am sure many tables were this Thanksgiving. There was Ferguson, there was Cosby, there was race and there was Obama. It was passionate, it was heated, it was tiresome, it was healthy – 4 hours later, and it was time for dessert. Pies and ice cream – all you can eat! We sat, we laughed, we reminisced and talked for hours until it was time to say goodbye for now. Abby called from Los Angeles, we passed the phone. It was Family, it was Thanksgiving.

Before I was to head back down to DC, Grandmama said they were going to see Aunt Carol and Uncle Woody down in New Jersey. I figured it would be a good break in the trip to stop and say hello before wrapping up the rest of the trip south. I hadn't seen them since our last family reunion some years ago. Uncle DK and I drove down in my truck while Grandmama

& Grandpa were in another car. It was good to spend that time with Uncle Dwayne. He and I as adults are far different than the 15 and 10yr old versions of us and the evolution is quite a good thing. I enjoy hearing his perspectives on life. He is a driven individual and passionate about his craft. When he wraps up his dissertation on the legacy of Broadway musicals & Race I will be eager to learn from his extensive research.

Aunt Carol & Uncle Woody moved last year from Union, NJ down to Columbus in order to be closer to cousin Wanda, her husband Andrew and their children Sean and Ashley. They have a spacious rambler in a 50 & over community that Aunt Carol had no problem raving about as she gave Uncle Dwayne and me the grand tour. Similar to Aunt Sandy & Uncle Bill's home, the history of our family stood at every turn. Graduations, weddings, family reunions, class pictures from days long past adorned the shelves -- faces young and old, all familiar, all Family. We sat and talked, we heard Uncle Woody wax poetic about how Santa never gave him the Red Ryder pump action, repeater BB gun he always wanted as a child. He lamented in great detail how the single shot BB gun he eventually received one Christmas was so poor in its execution and authenticity he could only shoot up into the air, as the single BB would simply roll down the barrel if he pointed the weapon downward after loading. It was a tale told so vividly and with such passion and angst that everyone in the room was nearly in tears as we ultimately decided *this* Christmas, Uncle Woody at 70+ years of age would get the repeater BB gun he so long desired. The ensuing debate over what channel the Florida State vs. Florida game was on was equally riveting. Who knew tensions could flare so high over whether or not the Verizon HD channels started at 600, 700, or 800. It was maddening and hilarious all at once. It was Family.

Girls, I wanted to get back to DC in order to see you, so I said my goodbyes, spoke with Grandmama and Grandpa about some of the things on my mind over the holiday and thanked them for being there and being supportive as the healing process moves forward. They are great that way. I hugged everyone and got on my way. Tank full, I headed south down 95.

Nearly home, not far past Baltimore at about 68mph, I felt the car jolt and sink to the ground. Instantly remembering every discussion I have had with

Grandpa about cars and accidents, as well as some actual experience I let off the gas, held the wheel tight and let the car slow on its own. I was able to maneuver the vehicle off an exit ramp. By the time I made it to the rear of the car, the wheel was facing a direction I didn't think a rear wheel could actually face unless you were driving a hook & ladder truck. Hello? USAA? Yes, I need some help. The flat bed tow truck arrived and I was pretty happy to see John and his son, Brendan. Brendan couldn't have been more than 10 years old, so to see him out there helping his Dad on a Saturday night was pretty awesome. The kid even knew his way around the levers, very cool.

It was almost midnight on Saturday and I didn't think twice about who to call. I called Family. I may have said 10 words to Cousin Skip before he calmly said that he was on his way. Cousin Skip left a holiday party to come and get me in Maryland. I was pretty damn glad to see him. We had a good laugh about the situation and he said something to me last night that I keep thinking about. "Be thankful the girls weren't out there with you and that something worse didn't happen." He was right. You girls were long in bed by then, safe and warm.

That truck got me up to New York for Thanksgiving in a snowstorm, brought your Grandparents and I to NYC for Thanksgiving and back home again, then Dwayne and I down to NJ to visit Aunt Carol and Uncle Woody – eventually getting me within 45 minutes of DC before it said enough. While I missed you this Thanksgiving girls, I am thankful you weren't in that truck last night. I am thankful you were safe at home – with Family.

#49

UPLIFT

Dear Basil & Sabine,

It's been a little while since I wrote you a letter and with the turn of a new season I figured now is as good a time as any to share a few things with you. Perhaps this letter will help me figure out a small situation. I have to help a friend. Actually, I *want* to help a friend. On the one hand it involves raising money; on the other hand it really means so much more. Let me provide you some background first.

A few years back when Daddy was feeling particularly down about his life, (*a self-pity party really*) I had several friends who made it their business to ensure I didn't let my head hang too far to the ground. One of those friends was Anthony Covington, Uncle Cov. Uncle Cov, in his own "not so subtle" way put his arm around me and said I needed to make my life right for me and more importantly *for the both of you*. He knows of what he speaks as Uncle Cov is raising two daughters of his own in Kennedy & Carter… aka your older sisters.

Familiar with my position and my feelings, he sat me down every so often and explained why it was tremendously important for me to ensure I got my priorities in focus and did absolutely everything I could to ensure you both never lost sight of how much I wanted to be present in your lives and just how much our conversations, meals, road trips and movie nights would actually mean over the course of your lives as you grow. He was spot on in his analysis as these little traditions of ours have become something I look forward to day in and day out. These are just a few of the things that keep me enjoying fatherhood. Even when Sabine spilled her untouched vanilla milkshake on the floor yesterday all I could do was smile to myself when the guy across from us said simply, "welcome to the club." I love the club. The one I am in everyday, not the one I used to be in every weekend.

Girls, you may find yourself in a position over your lifetime where a friend will see you struggling with something and will place themselves in a position of support if for no other reason than they *want* to be there for you. Accept this. Accept that you are worthy of someone's friendship; accept that you are worthy of the *good* in life. Uncle Cov knew I needed him during those moments and I am glad to have been in his line of sight. And now Uncle Cov needs me. Uncle Cov works for an organization called Big Brothers, Big Sisters of Maryland and he asked me if I would be on his team of bowlers as we help him raise money to benefit children who need the support of Big Brothers, Big Sisters. It is an organization that places adult mentors with children who can benefit from the guidance and friendship of strong individuals in their lives. So I have until this Friday to raise $200 for my bowling team. Now girls, last summer when you took it upon yourselves to have a bake sale out in front of the house to raise money for the homeless children who lived in DC and Haiti you did so because you passionately felt a desire to help someone whom you've never met and you knew could be helped through your energy and your willingness to *do something*. I hope I have learned from your example and can do the same.

Starting tomorrow, and each day this week I am going to write you a small letter to share with you a time in my life where someone helped me purely from their heart and not because they looked to gain anything from it. That is what being a friend is and that is what it means to perform a selfless act.

MORAL – Let your winter slumber allow for bountiful spring awakenings.

ꝗ

#50

Like a Good Neighbor

Dear Basil & Sabine,

As promised, I want to give you five examples of where I witnessed a selfless act or found myself on the receiving end of someone's generosity or kindness simply because they desired to help me along the way. I have come to find that these seen and oft times unseen actions whether man made or otherwise, can mean the difference between a big misstep, unfortunate circumstance or pure elation and satisfaction. It's a wide scale to say the least. Nevertheless, here's Monday's story:

You know how I have always reminded you of the kids Daddy grew with on his street all those years ago? If you go back to one of the letters I wrote to you on my way to 40 you will find one that speaks about a lot of those young friends I grew up with. Well, there are 2 names that I didn't mention in that letter, Michael Schwindeler and David Obreith. Michael came into the fold somewhat later down the road as he and his parents moved in some years after all of the older kids had been around for a while. He was several years younger than I was and a bit of a shy kid whose head seemed several years older than the rest of his body. I'll get back to him. Now David Obreith was a different animal. A year or two older than I, David was a bit of a maverick. If ever there was a 12 yr old version of MacGyver, David was it. While David and I weren't exactly the best of friends, I believe we had a bit of an understanding between each other. While I was making every effort to win my candidacy for President of Deer Run at the age of 11, David was cool with being someone I needed for a successful campaign but was clear he held no allegiance to anyone. I mean, he was 12. Nevertheless, David and I protected our street from any harm, you know, any kids from other streets that tried to bring their bikes onto our turf and pop wheelies better or build better jumps. We would have nothing of it.

Enter Michael Schwindeler. Now I made it my business to hawk Deer Run like a night watchman. I could tell you what most families were having for dinner on most any summer night on that street as I made my rounds. When the Schwindeler's moved in I scouted them out immediately. If memory serves I do believe I found myself questioning poor Michael almost immediately about where he was coming from and what his intentions were and just how big his matchbox collection was. And let's be clear, I was not bullying, I was inquisitive. There is a difference. Now Michael's parents, who still live in that same house, were actually rather quiet people, which I guess led to some of Michael's shy demeanor. But they were and still are very beautiful, loving people with a huge garden in their backyard by the way.

Now the previous family that had lived in the Schwindeler house had left an old basketball hoop in the driveway. Over the years, weather had gotten the best of the backboard and rim, but it still had a bit of life in it. Michael wasn't exactly the tallest guy on the block so the considerable amount of droop on the basket allowed him to hit his shots quite regular-ly. Well, one day when I was feeling pretty good about myself as I walked the cool pavement of Deer Run I ran across David who lived directly next door to Michael and we both meandered over to see Michael shooting hoops on that old hoop in the driveway. We both walked toward him, "Hey Mike, what's up?" I think Mike was just happy that we were over there trying to engage. He seemed happy to see us, for the moment anyway. He threw me the basketball as I took a couple of shots and then I looked at David and said, "Wanna see me dunk on that basket?" Of *course* they did.

Though I am not sure Michael wanted me to, and heck he may have even objected, but my mind was made up. I was going for two! And as I took a running start from the corner of the driveway, and the sold-out crowd of two screamed with anticipatory excitement and I became a slow motion Dr. J, I took the ball in my hands as I jumped from the ground and unleashed my inner Darryl Dawkins on that bad boy, completely ripping the rim from the wooden backboard – that it had, until now, been held to. I came down to the ground no longer with ball in hand, but with little piec-es of soggy wood around me and the metal rim on the ground. Michael looked devastated. David and I looked like someone was in trouble. In that moment I knew it was me. I immediately tried to explain to Mike that it was anything but my fault; I made an attempt at a Physics explanation and even somehow stated that perhaps he should have "warned" me that the backboard conditions were substandard. Horrible, I know. It was my fault and I knew it. And in the short amount of time it took for me to come up with the conclusion that I would have to face the music, the music was standing right in front of me. Yup, Mrs. Schwindeler, this otherwise quiet, demure woman came out of that garage like a bull down a street in Pamplona. Bellowing to no one in particular but directly to the three individuals standing amongst what was left of her son's basketball hoop in that driveway, she made it clear how she felt about the neighborhood welcome committee. I slumped back four houses down to my own drive-way and went to my room to await what fate would come my way once one of Mike's parents found one of my own. I was doomed. My candidacy was in serious jeopardy.

As I sat looking out that window the sun beginning to make its descent I could hear the faint sound of hammering coming from David's garage. *Bang, Bang, Bang...* over and over I could hear the sound of some serious work being done. I could barely make out what was going on in there but someone meant business. After a few more distinct noises I saw David emerge from his garage with the rim attached to a piece of new plywood. Could it be?!?! I ran out of the house and took off toward Michael's driveway. And there was David standing on a ladder putting this new, homemade, backboard contraption back onto the basketball hoop. I was filled with hope, glee and most of all relief that a butt-whipping was fading from my immediate future. By the time Mike's father got home, all concerned parties had retreated to their corners and cooler heads prevailed. Summer nights in upstate New York will do that to you. Suffice it to say, I never shot a basketball in Mike's driveway again and to this day every time I see his mother I say 'Hi' and keep it moving. David Obreith moved away from Deer Run and I never heard from him again, but I was damn glad to have him around when I needed him. He saved me that day.

MORAL – Learn to fix things, either with your hands or with your words; you'll need it someday.

#UncleCov

⅋

#51

Dear Basil & Sabine,

I was standing in the Pentagon courtyard yesterday listening to Afghan President Ashraf Ghani as he spoke to an assembled crowd about the totality of the war in Afghanistan. He spoke of sacrifice, he spoke of ideals and he spoke of Afghanistan standing on its own, not being a burden to America or the rest of the world. He also commented on the education of girls in Afghanistan and how at one point there were no girls in school across the country, but now the number was close to 3 million. This of course made me think of the two of you. And standing there in the crisp air I began to think about the sacrifice he spoke of – the sacrifice made by those of all nations involved who lost life and limb over the past 14 years. Loved ones lost, families devastated and lives turned around; and I began to ask myself at what cost? I may never have a full answer to that question, but in those moments as I stood there listening to this gentleman, oddly enough I began thinking of an individual I came across during my time in Kabul.

There was a particular young Army Specialist whose name I will not disclose in this letter, that's not important, what *IS* however, more important is how this cantankerous, rebellious and slightly out of order individual proved to me that kindness and selflessness come in just about all forms whether purposefully intended or not. His form, his demeanor were without compromise, uniquely his own. There are several people I served alongside at ISAF headquarters in Kabul who will remember this individual well, and make no mistake he was an 'individual.' He moved around the compound without much of a care in the world, and was not afraid regardless of rank to let you know just how he felt about *you* or most anything else he saw fit to speak on. In the military we often call that being on your *own* program. Looking back now, I think the Army and perhaps even the strain of deployments just got the better of this young man and he was ready to put it all behind him. This was something many of us could certainly understand. I know that you both along with so many other family members feel the strain of deployments just as hard and so the sacrifice President Ghani spoke of applies to you as well.

Oddly enough, the thing about this young man that struck me as I watched him day after day was his impressive ability to build furniture. It was amazing what this kid could do with the supplies he was limited to. The back of our work space was complete with picnic tables, benches and Adirondack chairs. In his own way he was actually making life away from home just a tad bit easier for all of us. Though I truly don't know if that was his aim at all; I think he just wanted something to do with his time without having to think about where he was. His efforts caught the eye of a female Canadian General who worked with us in the same building and had been working with local Afghan leaders trying to refurbish a school nearby. Considering the Specialist's penchant for woodwork she asked if he would build a number of desks for the school children to use if she was able to get the necessary supplies. He went to work immediately. For the last several weeks of his tour in Afghanistan, this tobacco-chewing, foul-mouthed, tool belt wearing Army Specialist cranked out some 30 desks for these Afghan students to use at this school. With the help of several of us on the ISAF staff a truck came one day and we loaded these desks and away they went. No fanfare, no cameras, just a small thing amidst a much larger picture of bigger things. Greater sacrifice, greater this, greater that. It's really not worth measuring quite honestly.

This past weekend Basil, you mentioned to me not to judge a book by its cover and you accurately explained what that phrase meant. Well, this instance is very much the same. Although Daddy wanted to "calibrate" this young man on more than one occasion for his lack of tact and respect for the chain of command, I allowed myself to sit back and observe where he was coming from and perhaps understand the *why* in his behavior. In the end he served his duty. He did so in his own way and was able to secure a legitimate place in the history of the bigger puzzle of helping to rebuild Afghanistan. Right now, somewhere in Kabul, an Afghan girl is studying at a desk this young man built - one amongst 3 million. What she learns at that desk may change the world. Believe that.

MORAL – Go to school girls, there is a desk there waiting for you to stand on and be heard.
#UncleCov

#52

Dear Basil & Sabine,

There are two sides to every coin and timing is everything. Listen carefully and I will explain what I mean. In my letter to you on Sunday (#49) I mentioned the catalyst for this string of particular letters, that they were centered on acts of kindness and generosity. I also made mention of the passion with which you sunk your teeth into raising money for orphaned children in Haiti as a result of the tragic earthquake there in 2010. Basil you were not quite 3 yet when that occurred, but when you were old enough to understand why Daddy was sent there you got it in your head to do something to help. This made me proud. It seems all last year you dedicated yourself in some form or another to either collecting clothes or funds to send there. This included the now infamous "BAKE SELL" out in front of the house last summer. And yes, we will do it again once warmer weather returns to earth or simply Washington DC, whichever comes first.

The tragic events associated with that earthquake were devastating to the people of Haiti despite millions of dollars raised and personal investments of emotion and time spent in aiding a rebuilding process. A process I am still not confident reached or were properly dispersed to those who needed it most. You'll understand this conundrum a bit later in life I'm afraid. Often times the best intended deeds and notions fall prey to those who would rather reap the benefits from the ill-informed or oppressed victims who are most deserving. I had the pleasure of working with numerous colleagues and knew several friends, Marnique Heath and Tiffany Carter specifically, who devoted their hearts and skills toward making a difference in the aftermath, and I am proud to know them.

Girls, it was important I lay that foundation out first for you both, so you understand THAT particular side of the coin, it is imperative you keep it first of mind for future endeavors. Now the other side – at some point it was time for Daddy to get home because someone had a 3rd birthday coming up and I just kind of wanted to be there for it. Also, there was something called Snowmageddon happening in DC and I was missing it! So one day a group of Sailors were given permission to rotate back to the United States and return home. I had a deputy in LT David Shark who was willing to stay behind and take the reins. Thank you David.

About 100 of us were taken to the national airport in Port-Au-Prince, still not yet open for commercial traffic due to repairs to the runway though we were to be taken home on a Navy aircraft. The buses dropped us off and we waited, and waited, and waited - several hours and no plane to speak of. We called back to our ship in order to get an update on what was happening only to find out the plane never left Florida due to maintenance issues. These things happen. Arrangements would have to be made for us to return to our ship or spend the night on the runway there in Port-Au-Prince. But then, as I said, timing is everything. Moments after getting word about our plane not arriving, we saw a much larger plane approaching the runway in the distance. Closer and closer it appeared with landing gear down. This sucker looked big. And sure enough, right then and there a Delta airlines plane landed on the runway and came to a stop about 100 yards from us. We watched as several people came off the plane and walked past us to awaiting vehicles. As it turns out an organization called Doctors Without Borders had chartered a flight to come and help with the victims of the earthquake. A few moments after those doctors and nurses left the airport a man in a white polo shirt and khaki pants walked over toward me and said, "anyone need a ride back to Atlanta?" I almost licked his face like a dog.

It took several phone calls to our Bureau of Medicine & Surgery command back in Washington to make sure we could all legally board that plane that afternoon, but in the end we all got onboard. I cried a bit as that plane took off looking down at what we were leaving and thinking about how many people could be looking up at us and wishing they could be on that plane. It's a tough pill to swallow and humbles you over and over to gain an understanding of just how blessed your life is in that moment. That man in the khaki pants and white shirt was Mike

Lowry, a representative of the airline. He made sure we were fed and that we were directed where to go once we landed in Atlanta. Though he went just a bit further -- I asked him about any flights going back to DC and once we landed that night we discovered one was about to take off. Mike called the gate for that aircraft and asked the pilots to wait; he then walked me to the plane and made sure I was onboard. I didn't lick Mike on the face but I looked him dead in the eye and said, "Thanks for getting me home man, it means more than you know." And I really enjoyed *that* Birthday party.

MORAL – Girls we don't ever talk to strangers, but if Mike Lowry shows up with a 747 and wants to bring you home to me, we're good.
    #UncleCov

ℛ

#53

Dear Basil & Sabine,
    Breaking Down. I could fill a 1GB hard drive with stories of break downs. Many of those would be vehicle break downs over the course of my years. The places, highways, turnpikes, and streets where I have found myself sitting off to the side, hazards flashing, hoping for a miracle and waiting on help – oh the agony of the break down. As I think back on my life I am reminded how Grandmama and Grandpa to this day have a constant con-dition of concern (*worry*) about the safety of their children once they get on the road. Some people call that particular condition Parenthood. It's written right there on the bill of sale. You just won't breathe a sigh of relief until you hear the key hit the front door. If I think I am worried now about a call from the school nurse about a playground accident, I have a whole new set of issues once I give you both the keys to the car.
    The breakdown however is not just reserved for the cars in our lives. There are other vehicles, boats, motorcycles, etc., but there is also the

breakdown of body, of marriage, of mental capacity, and the breakdown of self. What matters most, in my opinion when these "other" break-downs in life occur are the people who appear in your life to get you moving and back on the road again. I could fill another 2GB hard drive with stories of the people who helped me through the break downs in my life -- the people who won't just move on past without a glance or the people who won't ignore the warning sign of smoke coming from your place on the side of the road. It is in those precious moments where the simple kindness of an individual can make the difference in your life that will breathe faith back into your conscious. Kindness, can in fact give *you* life.

These acts are not always grand overtures however. It is a phone call, an arm around the shoulder, an email or written note. It may be stand-ing outside a Charlottesville courtroom today in support of a young man wrongly arrested, bloodied and bruised. It's being there when someone needs you if for no other reason than to show they are not alone. That may sound sappy and Pollyannaish but rest assured, though I do not wish for you to find yourself ever broke down on the side of life's road, I do wish for you an abundance of roadside assistance.

This particular string of letters are written in support of Tony Covington and his Big Brothers/Big Sisters bowling fund drive, so allow me to share with you a small story of how "Uncle Cov" helped me on the side of the road.

If you ever want to see a display of humanity and resolve run a mara-thon or simply watch one. Back in 2005 Daddy decided he was going to run the ING Miami marathon. I had trained for several months here in Washington DC from October to January (*cold months, keep that in mind*). By the time the date of the marathon arrived I was really very excit-ed and looking forward to completing a bucket list item. And how great was it to be in Miami of all places! I had a good night of sleep before the race, had the proper load of carbs prior to race time and planned out all of my water breaks and GU energy gel hits along the way. I was ready. The race began extremely early in the morning near American Airlines arena in downtown Miami. I set my watch, and slowly began moving forward to run my race. What a feeling?!

At about mile 6, feeling good and moving along at my pace I looked up toward a tower that had time and temperature on it, 7:06 am, 78 degrees. I could feel the frown on my face. Ummm, Daddy didn't train in warm weather like this. But I kept going. The people around you tend to keep you motivated in those early miles -- plenty of adrenalin to keep the blood moving. Oddly enough around mile 8, Daddy saw a familiar face cheering along the side of the road. I passed right by and then a couple of seconds later it hit me, "Hey, that was Covington." Right then, I made a very, very poor decision. I stopped, turned back a few steps and said, "Hey man, what's up, what are you doing here?" Dumb move. We chatted for a few moments, made plans to catch up later and then I started back up again. Momentum destroyed. I couldn't quite get my running rhythm back and it was only getting hotter.

Just after mile 14, water emanating from my pores like a fountain, I could hear my body, my mind and my heart were all having a conversation with one another. They were talking about how hot it was and how nice it would be to stop running and sit in one of those chairs the spectators were sitting in as I ran through Coconut Grove. I put the conversation on mute and somehow kept moving. By mile 19, the conversation was so darn loud I stopped and joined in for a little bit. I wanted to listen to them carefully, hear some of their reasoning. But then I looked around me and realized other people weren't breaking down so I should keep moving. Two miles later my vehicle needed roadside assistance and the tow truck was right there waiting for me. Uncle Cov had somehow made it up to that point in the race and decided he would stop doing what he was there to do and start jogging alongside me offering words of encouragement. Now to this day I couldn't tell you what he specifically said, I just know that his conversation was louder than the one going on inside of me and it quieted all the noise. So I kept running and before long he wasn't there, but I was still running and I eventually crossed the finish line.

Throughout your life you may have to pull over on the side of the road sometimes girls and you may have to call and wait for help, this is ok. You may need a jump, you may need a push, you may need a tow – you may simply need air for what's gone flat.

MORAL – Don't let the break downs outnumber the restarts; your engine will run again.

#UncleCov

৭৮

#54

Dear Basil & Sabine,

Well, here we are – I promised to write you 5 letters on kindness and acts of selflessness that have had an impact on my life in some way or an-other. Again, the letters in this string could have extended for quite some time as the ways in which I have been a beneficiary of someone's good grace extends on for a distance. The aim here was to shine a little light for Uncle Cov and help raise a few dollars for Big Brothers/Big Sisters in Maryland and just maybe at the same time provide you both with a few examples of kindness for your hip pocket. As I have expressed in previ-ous letters written to you, the notion that I would hope you both learn from the lessons and experiences I have had to endure such that you can make better choices and more informed decisions throughout your lives. However, I know that for you to truly learn, to truly live life you will in fact have to get out there and fly on your own someday. This I know all too well.

While I have sat here this week in front of my computer to relay to you these lessons in kindness I have continually asked myself where selfless-ness comes from; how does one find themselves enveloped with the in-nate ability to routinely put others before themselves in most any circum-stance whether big or small? From where does human decency begin its triumph of ignorance and hate? I have actually always known this answer, though having that knowledge does not always mean that it is automatically transferrable. For many this is a learned behavior; a conditioned response and from that point it develops into a choice really. Do I choose to live my life such that my actions can positively affect change in most all that I do? For some, that is a tall order; for others, not so much. To quote Damon Dash (*world's most prolific BOSS*) 'it's all in your perspective.'

Girls, Grandmama and Grandpa will always be my superheroes no matter who is in the room – you know why? Because all of their selflessness led to my life successes. It's quite true. And any act of kindness I witnessed from them had a profoundly impressionable impact on me. Here's why: It was my Mom who worked tirelessly at multiple jobs to save money for new clothes and Christmas gifts; it was my Dad who worked multiple jobs into late evening hours so we could ski and go to baseball games; it was my Mom who protected her students at Poughkeepsie High School by walking a gunman out of the school; it was my Dad who washed and cleaned Mr. Lawrence's car in our garage when he lost his daughter Michelle; it was my Mom who made sure we knew our worth so as not to be devalued by anyone; it was my Dad who would bring young children from the church out on the boat to give them a different perspective in life. It was my parents, girls. I learned by watching their example, I learned by watching the people, the community of friends and family they surrounded me with. This is how you learn selflessness, this is how you become familiar with the notion of kindness, the overwhelming sense of respect for an individual whom you know nothing of, but would wish to offer first the benefit of human decency unless shown otherwise. How different things would be if we led with this – what change could you affect? See: butterfly effect.

Several years ago, I was running down a DC street alongside Tony Horton (*celebrity name drop*) and we were having a conversation about the ability to help people. He said this to me, "Bash, if you had the ability to truly help people, would you do everything you could to make the most of it?" You just never know how great it could be, he said. Don't look for applause; just the satisfaction of extending yourself to uplift another is reward enough. Let that be your goal. Daddy didn't always think like this, not at all. My condition was bent toward the world of me. And I will tell you ladies as you get older you are going to find that the world of me is one empty, angry place to live. Though I don't suspect you will have that problem because I see in you open hearts full of love and respect. And through your family and the community we surround you with the **respect** you have within yourselves will always demand that in return. In this, be resolute.

I will wrap this one up now; it's Friday and 'Tonight, We Bowl!' (Grease 2 shout-out) I think we may have helped Uncle Cov out a little bit, at least I hope so. There will be more letters in the future girls, there's plenty more of life to learn from and to write about. In the meantime, go be superheroes little ones, go be superheroes.

MORAL – It *IS* perspective, make yours as wide as possible, you'll see more of what's around you.

#UncleCov

⚭

#55

A Fair Affair

Dear Basil & Sabine,

When you finally get around to reading this letter I will have taken you to close to 50 different fairs, carnivals, and theme parks. It's a youthful rite of passage. What is a childhood without funnel cake topped with confectionary sugar; iced cold, fresh-squeezed lemonade and soft-serve ice cream that drips from your chin in the humid night air, only to make you a sticky, face-painted child warrior ready for battle?

Now our last excursion to a county fair in summer of '14 was somewhat less than eventful. Minimal rides, a lame, duck race, no prizes won and an empty wallet later we retreated to the vehicle rather unimpressed, each bearing something similar to the *Kanye shrug. Like Opening Day of a new baseball season, the beginning of summer promises to bring forth a new set of rides and attraction, non-stop action. And right off the bat the DC fair was first on the list this past weekend set up right in the RFK stadium parking lot. So why not right? (*Let me tell you why not!*)

Now this is a fair, you have to set your expectations early. Just get it in your head that $100 is going out the door, never to return. It's the price of doing business. Once you get comfortable with that notion you will find yourself somewhat less frustrated as the Fair vacuum cranks on and starts to suck life from you. So let me just give you a bit of a play-by-play so that one day when you have your own children you are prepared for the 'Affairs of the Fair.'

When the woman at the ticket booth who amazingly can communicate without having one tooth in her mouth tells you that admission is $3 person and tickets for rides are separate, don't let intellect get the best of you here. Accept it and keep moving. Next, when she explains to you the option for purchasing unlimited rides versus paying for each individual ride, despite any other conventional wisdom you may have, gut-feelings or some keen intuition, just pay the $25 smackeroos per child. You're better off. OK, for those of you keeping score at home, that's $59 and we haven't quite taken 3 steps into the fairgrounds. What's that you ask? Oh yeah, parking. Well Daddy comes from a long line of descendants who know how to find free parking and then walk a country mile to wherever we need to be. This ensures a silent car ride on the way home (*Very important*). I digress.

Alright, well we're in – let's ride! Kiddie roller coaster to get our feet wet? No problem. Super Slide with the burlap rash? Why not?! The-Spin-So-Fast-Centrifugal-Force-Machine-With-The-Disappearing-Floor-That-Makes-Your-Head-Dizzy?? Yessss, Give it to me over and over!!!!! "Daddy, This.Is.Great!!!" And it *is* great, it's great for about the first 22 minutes and then you begin to come down from the high a little bit and start looking around at the other crazed fair-goers as you become immersed in all the bells, whistles, horns, music, smells, screams and carnival barkers on their microphones colliding in a cacophony of head melting madness. And on top of all it, you both are screaming at me with unbridled enthusiasm about what you each want to do next which is completely opposite of what the other wants Every.Single.Time - so I try to block it out. *(It's only temporary Bashon, get a hold of yourself.)* What will fix this situation before I transcend into a pathetic, overwhelmed Dad standing in a fairground parking lot, t-shirt wet with damp armpits, tears streaming down my face as kids jump and shout at either side? I know, funnel cake, stat! Yes, sugar will fix this situation. "Two funnel cakes please?" $14 Daddy-O! Thanks bro.

And so we press forward - sugar baby, let it seep into that bloodstream. Round 2 awaits. And as we move toward the back of the fair we venture into the realm of what I like to call – YOU MUST BE THIS TALL TO GET ON THIS RIDE. Now remember earlier when I was talking about the ticket agent with the *Choice Dental Plan. *(*Choice means you have a choice to use it or not)* Well what this individual doesn't explain to you is that while parents only keep track of their child's height in inches once a year when you put them up against that wall in your house on their birthday to draw the latest height line, The Fair Monsters love inches, they live by them. They keep a sign right there at the front of every line to show you how much they appreciate inches. Now, this year the magic number was "48. And while Basil was good to go at most every turn, Sabine you were doing some crafty foot and neck magic to make things work in your favor. I was duly impressed by your ability to grasp what was needed in order for you to gain an edge (*Daddy's Little Girl*). The lesson in this part of the story is that when you pay for unlimited rides at the front of the fair, you need to be aware that the height of your child may actually 'limit' the number of rides you can get on in the back of the fair. Noted. More stretching will be done before next summer.

Now, when rides are no longer grabbing ones attention, *fair games* come into play. And here are a few things to remember. Fair games are rigged. Can you win? Yes. Will you win? Not likely. You can get lucky and you can possess a little bit of skill, but for the most part you are walking away sullen and Daddy is walking away asking himself why the F*#$ he just shelled out $10 for 3 rings, $5 for 2 basketball shots, and $9 for 3 water pistol races. (*Anyone still counting here?*) And while we are talking about fair games and fair monsters here, let's focus on being FAIR. Cause make no mistake girls, there just *ain't* no room for fairness at the fair.

Toward the end of a night, most carnival barkers are trying to get you to come and spend your last few dollars before exiting for home. I get it. And since you have not won any sort of stuffed animal or blowup baseball bat yet, I am inclined to absolutely make sure my wallet is completely light and empty for the long trek back to the car. So let's walk over to those empty chairs over there for the water pistol race. Now I picked this one especially because there was no one else there and it promised to be a win for at least one of you. Good deal right? Yeah, right up until the selfish, 40-something year old woman with the bad hair and even worse vernacular sat her rump down next to a 6 and 8 year old shouting vehemently about how she wanted to win something before going home and proceeded to ace you both out of a prize with her water pistol acumen. You %#(@)$)!_#(@! - I stood there amidst the sticky air, fair sounds floating around me, eyes riveting back and forth in frustration, with your faces staring at me dejectedly asking, 'why didn't we win Daddy??' Instantly in my mind we turned those water pistols on her, saturating her bad weave and over-applied foundation with as much clean DC water as we could, short of waterboarding her. Really lady? I hope you get hit by the DC H street trolley... Oh wait. (*That's another story*)

And so, we walked away from fair follies into the darkening night. One last round of lemonade please for the country mile, $4 per cup. Admission, Tickets, Funnel Cakes, Lemonade x 2, Ice Cream, yeah that all costs money, it's the price of doing business. But the magic in those summer time fairs girls, the thing that makes it all worthwhile? It's the excitement in your voices before we even get to the ticket booth, it's hearing Basil's screams of joy when the ride takes off, it's wiping Sabine's tears when she runs into my arms after the haunted house, it's counting water bugs disappearing into sidewalk cracks on the way back to the car; it's me eating the funnel cake you ask me to hold while you go on the next ride and reminisce about the days I spent at the Dutchess County Fair when I was little. And well, that's fair.

MORAL – Don't do the math, it won't add up.

⚘

#56

Grandmama's Fight

Dear Basil & Sabine,

Grandmama has cancer, breast cancer. We weren't quite sure at 6 & 8 just how or when to tell you, though I now believe children are likely better at handling this news than most adults - I think it's your current lack of height that helps keep you grounded. There are however, a few important things we want you to understand and consider as we all move forward. Grandmama is fighting every day and she is doing it with the undying love and support of friends, family and her church community combined with an unwavering faith in God. What you may not know at this young age is just how much your presence in her life is helping to give her strength and determination to stand up and face her diagnosis; rising above the pain and the glaring statistics associated with breast cancer in women.

As I write this letter to you Grandmama has 1 more chemotherapy session remaining before she begins moving into her radiation phase of treatment. She has spent a great deal of the past few months either in bed or very close to home, venturing out with Uncle DK and Grandpa only as her energy would allow. Your visit over Memorial Day weekend 2015 gave her joy beyond words. We tried to hide as much as we could from you during the visit so as to ensure we kept smiles on everyone's faces and your questions to a minimum (*silly us*). I believe your inquisitive nature and humorous reaction to Grandmama's wig was a clear indication that you are more than capable to handle whatever news may come in your direction -- "do you sleep with that on?" – Sabine.

Girls, Grandmama is the rock of our family. She is the one we lean on in times of pain, sadness and frustration. She is the first to share our joys and the last to ever leave our sides no matter what the situation may bring. For the first time in my life as I watched Grandmama face her surgery with Grandpa at her side I realized how much I took for granted what that rock means not only to me, but to her family, friends and colleagues. I was confronted with the stark reality of just how much we rely on the presence of that rock and its firm, unwavering hand upon all of us. She's *always* there. So why would I think any of that would change? Today, as I watch Grandmama use the same will and fortitude she has carried for all of her life to confront cancer head-on, I see so clearly just how the battle waged in the face of cancer is not defined by winning or losing – but rather it is rooted in the decision you make to live. And live with no boundaries; fearlessly, unrelenting and with the top down to feel the breeze.

Grandmama has chosen to *live*. She lives to laugh; she lives to love; she lives to continue her work; she lives to spend her time with family – with **you**. Linda Melton Mann, your grandmother, lives so that her life means infinitely *more* to others around her who stand to benefit from her love and support in any manner she is able to render it. And so girls, we have a charge. Our charge is to not just call Grandmama on the phone or FaceTime on the weekends or visit Grandmama and give her all the hugs we can. Our charge is to live our dreams. Our charge is to face our fears courageously. Our charge is to love family and be forgiving in our hearts. Our charge is to live with an undying faith in God. Our charge is to live with a **robust** self-love and give of ourselves unselfishly.

She wants you to know her #cure rests in her commitment to live #MANNSTRONG. It is a commitment she defines by using her life's work to pay it forward. We honor her commitment by the manner in which we live.

And so I will walk, I will run, I will swim, I will crawl, I will speak, I will write, I will love -- to *live* for my Mom who has cancer; cancer does not have her.

ॐ

#57

Daddy's Not Young Anymore

Dear Basil & Sabine,

I'm getting older and here's how I know. It all started off easy enough. Sunday morning, big breakfast, eggs, bacon, griiiiiiiittttss! Get everyone showered, dressed, lotion on the legs and elbows and we are out the door. Birthday party starts at 11am in Rock Creek Park and I want to get us there on time. Easy ride through our nation's capital, past the monuments, plenty of people out running and biking, ahhhh today's going to be just like Ice Cube said it would. Arrive at the party for 6yr old Zeke right on time, even a tad early (*military execution*).

Typical outdoor party - you got your 3-legged race, scavenger hunt, balloons, snacks and drinks for the kids, beer and wine for the adults, the obligatory birthday party standard food of choice – pizza and cup-cakes, add a little sunshine after a tsunami of rain the previous day; insert screaming kids and you got yourself a successful little birthday soiree. Victory! It was a nice little break from the indoor, moon-bounce jumping factory that drives every parent to comment on why they are in the wrong business. Cool. I mean, what could make it any better right? Hahaha! I'll tell you what – Motherf@#*!'n water balloons!!! 150 of 'em. Way to go Fred! Good call. Or so I thought.

Now you see, what is it that will drive kids and adults into the ul-timate panorama of giddiness and euphoric tumult? Yup, the sight of water balloons! You can literally feel the energy start in your toes and move toward your fingertips as you gear up for the ultimate challenge of search & destroy. Being responsible, patient parents we kept the kids at bay, their mouths foaming with frothy delight in anticipation of what was about to ensue. They were 4-foot warriors ready for battle. Your Auntie Kim, a calculating, measured Super Mom steeped in the laurels of academia had laid out a plan for fairness and calm (*yeah, ok*). That lasted about 2 minutes until her husband Fred let out his inner Cujo! All at once the environment reached a fever pitch. Kids unleashed, moms moving away to safe distances, seeking dry land – It was *on* like Donkey Kong! This was war and there would be no prisoners. Fred was moving like a man possessed. He didn't care – any child, Jew or Gentile was fair game. He gathered balloons in his hands with the dexterity of a brick layer, cradling them in multiples like a farmer carrying eggs to market. I watched with baited captivation from a safe distance. Though the familiar spark of energy was soon climbing up my legs; I could feel the impulse drawing me into the scrum. No longer could I remain on the sidelines. It was pulling me in like Al Pacino to a family commitment. And then, all at once I found myself motivating with swift abandon toward the bucket full of balloons – eyes pierced, fixated on my goal.

I weaved toward the bucket, advancing with military-grade precision; gathering up as many hefty balloons as my hands would hold. I knew my extract had to be quick. Fred was looming large like an Allied tank division commander standing ready at Bastogne. He was making his presence felt across the battlefield as 6yr old after 7yr old was left wet, crying in tears from his onslaught salvo and pin-point accuracy. Balloons clutched to my chest I sprinted toward my outpost. A cheesy, Cheshire cat grin planted across my face, scampering through the wind as I felt the child-like glee filling me up inside. And then it happened...

Moving at a high rate of speed throughout my escape, the soles of the size-13 Men's Keen "Daddy sandals" I had on were rendering minimal support to my 200lbs. + frame upon the damp, loose ground. As I felt myself losing balance I instinctively executed the absolute wrong move as I tried to feign off embarrassment by attempting to catch myself from the fall. It was one long, exaggerated lunge after another as I grew closer and closer to mother earth; I could feel all sense of grace and dignity slipping from my grasp. And then, there I was; suspended in mid-air no longer able to stand upon my own two feet. I barrel-rolled upon the ground like a Texas lawman wildly chasing a teenager from a pool (**MESSAGE!**), as the entirety of my back from my neck, shoulders and hind parts made solid contact with the unforgiving ground. I somehow miraculously found myself back upon my feet standing erect with a stunned look of suspense upon my face, looking to the adults in the crowd for some type of reaction. Most just staring back in silence with a look of uneasy pain, horror, and disbelief upon their faces attempting to digest what unfolded in front of them. The East German judge gave me an "8.5" for flawless execution and sticking the landing. I knew almost immediately something was amiss however.

Shaking off dirt, dust, and cool points I valiantly fought on – standing in one place as I unleashed the balloons that somehow survived my Triple Lindy. With each throw I had to admit to myself that I had perhaps damaged more than my soul with the fall. It would be some time later that I found myself in front of a doctor wondering aloud why walking and sneezing were so painful. Easing myself out of bed allowing feet and hands to hit the floor at the same time, the pain causing quiet, man-like whimpers as I attempted the easiest of daily tasks. Days later in my mind's eye I can still see a slow-motion cascade of laughing faces from every young kid at that party holding a water balloon, prepared to strike; Fred Jones standing behind them leading the mockery!

And yet, there *IS* a lesson in all of this. Though the child within you need never take leave of your core, your essence, your soul - may you never forget that the swift recovery of childhood injury does *not* translate at the age of 41.

⚘

#58

Stealing Home

I understand the "why?" -- I do. Whether drugs, money or even the sheer thrill, I understand why people steal. Doesn't mean I condone it or even makes it easier to swallow when it smacks you in the face -- I'm simply saying I understand the dynamics surrounding the action. However, my larger issue, my conundrum if you will, unfolds in two distinct lines of thought; one albeit, a tad more nuanced than the other.

Let's look at the first one, as it's a bit more straightforward. It's the inconvenience factor surrounding the steal. Considering this was a relatively minor offense in my opinion, as I could have walked outside this morning and found that *no* car was sitting in the driveway at all, right? So, now that I have had time to sit still and take a mental account of items "relieved" from the vehicle I can assess this as a crime of minor inconvenience to my life. Now I presume most people will say that I should in fact be grateful to have arrived at this juncture. I mean, what with everything else going on in the world and the fact that things could always be worse. You hear that a lot. And it's the right sentiment, it makes sense. I get it. I really do. Am I disappointed? Sure. Unnerved a skosh? Perhaps. But honestly, a couple of phone calls here and there, a trip to Target, Sprint, Apple, and an online purchase or two from Amazon.com and I am pretty much back in business. Cool.

But now I arrive at the second piece of the equation; appropriately named the #2. This is the more involved issue at hand when faced with The Steal. You see, I am a reflective, layered individual. I think too long about the matters of the day, allowing them to linger on my brain. I am a man who buries frustration, anger, and stress deep down within my body because I embrace hypertension for the immeasurable joy of it. Part of my problem is that The Steal is typically my own fault. I have to accept this. Insurance companies should avoid me like the plague. I feel safe in places I shouldn't. You know, like home. This is the second time in four years this has happened, both occurring at **home**. I have only myself to blame. Perhaps you're familiar with my plight. You come home after a long day, you have the kids in the car, and you have an assortment of bags to bring inside. Someone inevitably has to use the bathroom and you can't get to your keys fast enough for *that* issue to be resolved so once you get the front door open and everyone inside you can see where remembering to lock the car door isn't necessarily first of mind. And, when dinner needs to be cooked and there is a bottle of red waiting for you on the counter the vehicle sitting in *your* driveway becomes a fast, fading memory; as do the personal items inside of it.

The crux of the problem is that while most all those "items" can be replaced, there are always going to be one or two things that can't. Like the camp project the 6yr old was so proud of sitting on the front seat, the notes you carried with you in your bag (habit) from loved ones so you would always have them close, the ticket stub from Derek Jeter's last game you attended that you meant to have framed but just never got around to it that you kept in the glove compartment. Those ain't coming back buddy. So I'm left to stew over the violation of the steal and how I can really only look at myself and shake my head a bit in a Fred Sampson, 'You Big Dummy' kind of way.

The reason it's nuanced is because me being me, I won't let it go. I'll hang on to this for years. I'll peruse my neighborhood like 'McGruff' the crime dog, staring intently at anyone I think may have my property. I'm just built that way - a tad off center and downright foolish at the wrong times. I wish I could point to this as a case of masked bravado, but I know full well if I see someone with that bag no matter where I am or who I am with, I will stop what I am doing and interact with this individual in a way that will be emotionally charged, ignorant and fool hardy. It's not good practice. In the moments afterward the part of me that knows I was wrong will immediately try to amend the actions in my mind, excusing it as a sort of vigilante justice. In the end however, it is my hope that the greater human, the 'better Bashon' in me will persevere and resolve to accept whomever the individual was who stole from me gets greater use from those items than I ever could have. I hope one day they won't have to resort to The Steal. I search myself daily for that humanity.

Though, until I am awash in that spirit of humanity I am left to face the flip side of the coin. The anger I feel at the violation I am faced with. And despite understanding the clear, inherent consequence of spreading bad energy into the universe, there remains in me a desire for five minutes in a room with this individual, and that's just sad.

"But I'm trying Ringo; I'm trying *real hard* to be the Shepherd." (c) Jules Winfield

♃

#59

Back to School

Dear Basil & Sabine,

There's something to be said for the authentic newness of returning to school. While it signals a close to the fun and sun of summer break, it also ushers in a new chapter of evolution. You are each evolving along your educational spectrum, a new school year, a new grade, a new opportunity for learning. The learning part is integral to life. It's primarily the reason why school is so essential to your success – you are in fact there, to **learn**. But it is also important to note that we learn just as much *inside* the classroom doors as we do before we even walk through them.

Let's take today for instance. Earlier this morning you both learned who would become your teachers for this new school year and also who of your friends would be alongside you *learning* each day. Now Basil you made it quite clear to us that if you did not get the teacher you desired or the 'friend' you wanted in your class this year, someone was going to be made to pay. You were going to wear your anger out in the open. And well, upon hearing the unfortunate news this morning on both fronts that you would in fact have a teacher other than whom you had hoped and you would have to endure another year without Cameron, I could hear in your voice the disappointment you held inside. For this I do apologize. As a parent and former 3rd grader, you have my sympathy and understanding.

But alas, do not be completely disheartened my child. For this too, shall pass. I have it on good authority that while you will have to endure your daily classroom hours without the presence of Cameron and several of your other friends; you will have countless opportunities to excel in the classroom with minimal distraction from *close* friends. You will be focused, determined and eager to raise your hand without the threat of sidebar conversations and the silliness of potential 9yr old jocularity shared amongst girlfriends. These particular instances of camaraderie will in fact be held in abeyance and shared during the more intimate and less arduous time of day – afterschool. I mean just think, 3 hours of uninterrupted time outside of the classroom dedicated to play, conversation, secrets, silliness, and giddiness. You know, KID-ness. And better yet, this doesn't even include the 137 playdates, sleepovers and birthday parties you are going to experience with Cameron over the course of the school year that we as parents just *love* between our tired Friday nights and peaceful Sunday afternoons. While some may say there are no guarantees in life, Basil I am going out on a limb here to say you have a just a bit more than a 'Ronda Rousey' fighting chance of having your fair share of Cameron time.

Look, I understand the hurt and the disappointment, I really do. At your age I know the world tends to revolve around your friends and what's for dessert. Truth be told, it has a lot to do at my age too, so at least you have that to look forward to. But I will tell you girls, if I spent every school year with the same group of friends and the teacher I always "thought" was the best for me, I would never get to experience what truly was best. And while I don't expect you to quite understand this now, trust me when I say that you are going to gain a much richer experience from widening the group of friends in your life's classroom as you grow older. It allows you the chance to see the world from different angles and process more of what is out there. You will be better because of the variety in your teachers and not simply looking for the fun one. Fun is easy. We want intriguing and mind-opening. That's where the learning begins.

MORAL – Smile and let Mom & Dad take the first day of school picture. As your parents, we enjoy the evolution of **you**. It's a good ritual.

⚘

#60

Struggle

Dear Basil & Sabine,

Not long ago I found myself sequestered amongst an assortment of Navy colleagues for a symposium in the field of public affairs. Some of these individuals I had close relationships with, others I had known from our professional interactions over years gone by. Many of them I consider friends, more so than colleagues. As I was milling about and catching up with familiar faces I was approached from time to time by one or two people who wanted to offer a bit of thanks for what I have shared in these letters. (*BREAKING NEWS – these letters went a little bit farther than just the two of you.*)

I was struck by what each of these individuals had to say; it was a sincere Thank You for sharing my/our story. As I hung my head a bit and looked toward the ground, unsure of how to respond to the compliment, one woman whose words forced me to raise my head, looked me square in the eye and said, "it's no longer about you." Her words were penetrating. After driving home, staring out the window and contemplating what this woman said, I conceded she had a point. As I look back over the course of this 'lovenotes' journey I don't suspect I ever truly intended for it to be about me, as I wanted **you** to benefit from the lens I saw through in the hopes it would one day make your view clearer. Her words were a defining declaration – this helps someone.

Girls, people love a good story. They love an underdog, a comeback, a champion; they love a good love story. What you don't hear much of however is the story so many of us will go through every day of our lives -- the story of struggle. Most people are loathe to share their personal struggles. There are plenty of reasons for this. For many it's a flat out, 'none of your business' concept. Private matters deserve to sometimes be just that, private. Though what I am referring to are the people who could benefit from undoing the burden of personal struggle; whatever they may be. It is my belief often times people feel ashamed of their struggle(s) or are scared to share what pains them for fear of injecting even **more** pain by making it an exposed reality. The truth, my truth anyway, is the eye-opening freedom of self-discovery found by accepting and embracing my own struggles and not being afraid to admit my flaws not just to myself but to those around me. But it is a *daily* exercise, knowing the first part of the equation lay in facing and admitting to the pain, insecurity and weakness that brought you to wherever struggle finds you.

Daddy has and will struggle with sobriety. Daddy struggles with the weight of not being the best husband he could have been. Daddy struggles with the insecurity of not being liked by people who do not care much for me. Daddy struggles with placing Happiness as a value directly proportional to material wealth. This is a part of **my** story. I accept it. But it doesn't define my life story. There are far too many other pieces of my story board that are infinitely more important to what makes me get up in the morning and fight those struggles. They are family, they are true friends, they are self-worth, and they are the two of you. I will wage war with those struggles as long as it takes to ensure I am present for all of the *good* in my life and continue to let the story unfold, wherever it may lead.

I have a good deal of wants for you both. But most of all I want for you to appreciate and love your **own** stories – and all that makes them unique to you. Each of you has the greatest stake as the chapters unfold. Your stories will have ups, downs, agony, and elation, plus a million other twists, turns, and surprises. Don't be afraid of it. Face it bravely and without hesitation. If you do this, I promise that one day as you look through the pages you will have discovered you achieved the E.G.O.T of your own life story.

MORAL – Cast your eyes up from the ground, you'll like what you see in front of you.

With an overabundance of Love,
Your Father

ॐ

-CLOSING TIME-

Made in the USA
Columbia, SC
01 March 2018